SOME REASONS FOR WAR

SOME REASONS FOR WAR

How Families, Myths and Warfare Are Connected

by Sue Mansfield and Mary Bowen Hall

THOMAS Y. CROWELL NEW YORK

Library of Congress Cataloging-in-Publication Data
Mansfield, Sue.
  Some reasons for war.

  Summary: Presents theories based on human psychology of why we
have wars, tracing the history of war from Neolithic times to the present.
  1. War—Juvenile literature.   2. Military history—
juvenile literature.   3. Peace—Juvenile literature.
[1. War.   2. Military history] I. Hall, Mary Bowen.
II. Title.
U21.2.M343 1988   303.6'6   87-47694
ISBN 0-690-04664-2
ISBN 0-690-04666-9 (lib. bdg.)

Contents

Introduction

How can we study war?

We can't pin it down and dissect it like a flower blossom or a frog. Nor can we set up a laboratory experiment and make tests—as we might with an unknown chemical—to analyze its properties. The study of war, because of its nature, is not a science. On the contrary, the study of war was described by Karl von Clausewitz, one of the great strategic thinkers about warfare, as an "art."

While we can't study war by dissection or experiment, we can collect a great deal of knowledge about it by studying the warfare of the past—including the very recent past. This knowledge comes from several sources: historians, studying the written records left by previous generations; anthropologists, studying the wide variety of human societies existing in the world; and sociologists, studying the social and cultural backgrounds and the actions of men and women who make war.

These are not the only people who study war. Military experts, for example, study wars in order to learn *how* they have been fought. They examine and compare the details of past battles in an attempt to understand which tactics and strategies are most likely to succeed. They need, therefore, histories that are as accurate as possible. For them, the past can be the equivalent of a careful laboratory experiment waiting to be analyzed.

Other people have studied war in order to discover *why* humans engage in warfare, hoping that a better understanding of the motives that lead people to wage war will make it easier to avoid war in the future.

Some of these researchers, for example, have studied war by combining the data and methods of economics with the data of military history. Their studies have shown how different economic systems affect the size and character of warfare, and how the economic demands of war affect societies. These researchers have also been able to suggest some of the economic reasons—desire for gold or spices or territory—that have led certain individuals or groups of people to become very warlike.

Political scientists, on the other hand, investigate how military organizations are connected to the branches of government: legislative, judicial and executive. They study the conscious decision-making processes that have led to declarations of war, and the kinds of political considerations that may have led rulers to be militarily aggressive.

Another approach to the study of warfare involves psychology—the emotions, habits and beliefs, both conscious and unconscious, that help determine the actions of individuals and of groups. This psychological approach tries to explain why some individuals are brave and others cowardly, and also why some individuals and societies are very violent and aggressive while others are peaceful.[1]

The research on which this book is based, however, was brought about by a very specific insight: *the recognition of a close parallel between certain kinds of warfare and certain kinds of family structures and ways of raising children.* This research shows that different family and child-rearing patterns have been responses to changing patterns of getting food and other material necessities of life.

Why should these changes have led human societies to invent war, or—at various times—radically change its nature? Psychology investigates the ways in which adult behavior has its roots in childhood experiences. Since warfare is the result of complex adult behavior, a psychological approach is perhaps the best way to study how warfare began and how it has evolved. This book therefore explores family structures and the way children are raised in different societies in relation to how these societies wage war.

It is important to remember that anyone who studies war will be dealing with theories. Theories pull together and attempt to make sense of selected pieces of infor-

mation. (But theories about how the world works are—
or should be—always subject to testing.) Yet no single
approach has pulled together all the available information about warfare; no one has developed one comprehensive theory that satisfactorily combines all the insights
and ideas developed by scholars in different areas.

We have made certain that the facts on which this
book is based are the most accurate available, tested and
"proven" by historians, anthropologists and sociologists. And we have taken into account many other factors—political, economic, even literary and religious—
although, admittedly, we have not given these other
factors as much weight or attention as the psychological.
Also, this book does not present all possible knowledge
about warfare. We cannot guarantee that this book presents the "whole truth." Our theories are just that: theories.

People everywhere must try to understand the reasons
for war and take constructive action, based on what they
believe, to help avoid its destructive consequences. The
study of war, while as much art as science, must nonetheless be based on information. We hope our readers
will go on to do their own *individual,* creative thinking
about this devastatingly important part of human life.

Sue Mansfield
Mary Bowen Hall

Chapter One

Myth and Reality

A young man is standing on a high bluff, or perhaps an open walkway atop an infinitely tall structure. He's far above the earth, and seems to be waiting for something to happen. A breeze riffles his hair; his handsome face is tense and his hand moves nervously on the weapon he wears at his waist. "For you, Oliver," he whispers.

Quite suddenly the opponent the young man has been waiting for arrives. He is large and dark, with a cruel face.

"Well," he sneers, "are *you* really the best defense your people can produce?" Then he laughs menacingly. "This will be another easy victory, just as it was easy to dispose of your puny friend Oliver. And then you and your people will meet the fate you deserve!"

Our hero's eyes flash with anger.

"How dare you mention Oliver's name! You know you were able to kill him only by trickery. But my people will remember and honor him long after you and your kind have been banished into darkness!"

As he speaks, the hero pulls out his weapon and prepares to attack his loathsome enemy.

"The first blow will be for you, Oliver," he whispers. And he vows silently to fight to the death for his friend's memory. Even if he himself is killed, Oliver's dying will be avenged.

The setting may be in the distant future, filled with star fleets and imaginative technology, or in a magical past, with castles and wizards and fantastic beasts. It may also take place in the American Southwest, in which case there will be bloodthirsty Indians, renegade outlaws or cruel Mexican bandits.

Almost anyone who knows popular movies and books should recognize this story. It's so familiar we can easily fill in the background—the kinds of events that have led up to the duel between the hero and his opponent—and know, in general, the outlines of the rest of the tale.

The hero is not only handsome, he is "good." He is kind to children and animals, and respectful toward women. He is faithful to the laws and ideals of his people, who are kindly and courageous. Though he and his people yearn for a peaceful future, the hero justifiably wants revenge for his friend's death and for the ills everyone has suffered at the hands of the enemy.

The enemy is not only ugly, he is almost inhuman. He may, in fact, be half animal or half machine. He represents the forces of darkness, and he will speak of taking revenge for slights he imagines he has suffered in the past but which we know to be petty. He will be arrogant and vain.

Both hero and villain want glory. The villain, however, is incapable of pursuing it in a chivalrous and honorable fashion. Moreover, he is the leader or the chief fighter of a deadly and expansive force, one that is attempting to enslave or destroy the people represented by our hero. The villain represents a cruel and greedy people, insatiable in their need for power and control—sadists who enjoy trampling on the weak.

In an old-fashioned cowboys-and-Indians Western seen on late-night television, however, the story may be different. The hero may be the chief fighter for a young civilization, selflessly attempting to establish law and order in an "untamed" land. The villain will be fighting for a barbaric people, too superstitious or vicious to recognize the benefits they are being offered. Which side is good and which is evil depends on who is telling the story.

In any case, there will be clearly defined and identifiable "good guys" and "bad guys." Both sides will fear destruction and annihilation. But the villains usually will be depicted as having a choice: if they were not so greedy or so uncivilized, they would be left alone. On the other hand, the good people will find themselves in such a frightening, dangerous situation that they feel they must eradicate the forces of evil that threaten them in order to survive.

The hero will fight desperately but bravely to protect his people from evil. The forces he confronts will seem quite powerful. More than that, they will be crafty and deceitful in their strategies.

But the hero will win.

He will then return to his people, battered but triumphant. He will receive the acclaim of his rescued nation and be reunited with the beautiful woman—perhaps a princess—whom he loves. And, at the end of the story, there will be a touching scene when he attends a memorial service for his dead friend.

The "evil ones" will have been banished forever—unless a sequel is planned. The "good people" will settle down to enjoy prosperity and harmony, but they will remain continuously aware that the price of a peaceful future is preparedness for battle. Very likely, there will be an inscription on Oliver's tomb to remind them of this.

Such a story can be very entertaining, especially if it is well filmed or written and full of unusual characters and unexpected events. Watching it is exciting. We enjoy such adventure stories because they take us, temporarily, into a world that is much more emotionally satisfying than the actual world of our everyday lives.

The workaday world in which we normally live is, unfortunately, rather complex. "Good" and "bad" are usually mingled in the characters and actions of our friends, parents, teachers or employers; our own best intentions and actions often produce unclear results. Also, because major events in our lives are usually the result of hundreds of little conflicts or thousands of individual decisions and acts rather than isolated moments of danger, excitement and heroism are rare and difficult to achieve.

The world of adventure stories is much simpler. The good and bad are unmistakably identified; correct action is easy to define. Unpleasantness and pain are caused by evil forces that are, at least by the end of the story, defeatable.

These stories tell us that a single individual can, with courage and skill, determine the fate of the universe. We know before the story begins that the good are going to triumph and live happily ever after. In our pleasure at that outcome, we may fail to notice another prevalent message: Happy endings and peace can be achieved only through warfare and violence.

Everyone knows these stories are not true. The characters, the plots, perhaps even the settings, have been invented. They have never really existed, except in the minds of writers, directors and actors—and the audience.

Unfortunately, however, there is another sense in which we may believe that this celluloid adventure story *is* true. Even though we realize that the plot is imaginary, through endless repetition and variation we may come to believe that it nonetheless reflects an accurate picture of how the universe works. In the end, we may come to expect our leaders to act like the heroes in these stories. Indeed, the "good guy/bad guy" story, repeated in a thousand different locations and versions, has become a modern myth.

What, exactly, is a myth?

Sometimes we use the word "myth" to refer to a specific kind of story—in particular, the stories about the gods and goddesses of ancient Greece or Rome or Babylon. Obviously a twentieth-century film is not a myth.

But we also use the word to distinguish among different kinds of thinking. There are scientific and philosophical ways of thinking, and there is also a mythic mode of perceiving reality.

Sometimes the word is used in this sense as if it were another word for "lie" or "untruth." To say a statement is "just a myth" is to suggest that it is false, that it has no basis in fact. That is because in our conscious minds we confuse "fact" and "truth." We have come to accept and believe in scientific means of discovering and stating "truths." We expect our fact seekers to be objective, and we want their conclusions to be stated in an unemotional manner—if possible, in mathematical equations or scientific formulas. The scientific method requires information to be presented this way so that it can be tested and verified by others.[1]

The truth asserted by a myth, on the other hand, is not arrived at by objective experiments. Rather, mythic truth derives from a strong emotional response to a personal experience. It is an emotional truth, like "I am angry," or "I wish the world were peaceful." These are true statements, even if they cannot be quantified—put into equations or formulas—or tested.

A myth attempts to convey an emotional truth that

is recognized and felt by more than one person. In order to make the truth more general, the emotion is expressed in the form of a story. Such a mythic story can be distinguished from "mere" fiction by the fact that it claims to tell a general truth about the human condition or the nature of reality. Its truth, moreover, is confirmed—when it conveys a widely shared emotion—by the response of the listener or reader. Its power depends not on its factual accuracy but on its emotional convincingness.

Centuries of belief in a single deity have robbed most of the older myths about gods and goddesses of their ability to rouse our emotions. They have become simply interesting "museum pieces," part of educated literary knowledge. But there are some very old mythic stories which, because they do not involve gods and goddesses, have kept a place in our cultural life. Consider, for example, the old myth that babies are brought by storks.

It is unlikely that anyone over the age of five has ever believed that this story was literally true. Even the most unscientific people have realized that women become pregnant; they know the baby grows inside the mother and then the woman gives birth.

But the mythic story about the stork conveys an emotional truth. It reflects a very ancient and widespread feeling that a healthy new baby is a gift from nature—or God. The stork myth has validity because of the emotions—gratitude and happiness—that the birth of a healthy baby usually evokes from adult humans. (Of course, the brothers and sisters of this new baby may not share this feeling. For them he may be just a squally bother and a competitor for the attention and love of their parents!)

Even with the most advanced technology, conception and a successful delivery are events that humans cannot completely control. Adults still feel a sense of awe and gratefulness. And so our society has continued to "use" the myth of the stork to convey that emotion; stork pictures are associated with going to baby showers and celebrating the baby's birth. The picture of the stork on a birth announcement is expected to evoke a response: a shared happiness that will be expressed through the giving of a gift.

This response to the picture of a stork illustrates another aspect of myths. When a myth is "true," it calls forth an emotion, and such emotions normally express themselves through action. When we are happy, we want to laugh; when we are sad, we want to cry; when we are angry, we want to shout and bunch up our fists. Since the emotion evoked by a myth is a shared or communal emotion, it typically leads to communal action—a religious ritual or a baby shower.

The ancient Greeks, for example, expressed their sense of delight and pleasure in the wine they made from grapes by a story about the god Dionysius who, they said, had brought them the grape. According to the story, Dionysius had a very eventful life: at one point, in fact, he was hacked to death by women he had trusted. But he was also reborn. Thus Dionysius was like the grape vines that every fall had to be pruned and every spring burst forth into leaf. But the story of his tragic death also conveyed the emotional truth that wine was both a blessing and, if used unwisely, potentially dangerous. At least twice a year—at planting and harvest times—the emotional truth was acted out in all Greek cities in great—and rather drunken—celebrations that allowed everyone to share the emotional ecstasy and the tragic potential of Dionysius and the grape vine.

Myths, therefore, not only present an emotional rather than an "objective" truth; they also call for action. A scientific formula presents information. A myth, on the other hand, calls for bringing about the truth it proclaims.

What does all this have to do with warfare? Just as humans have created stories about the stork to convey an emotional truth about birth, they have created myths about the origins and purposes of warfare. Such stories—based on shared emotions of anger, greed or fear—are attempts to explain why people have fought in the past.

War myths convey what different societies have believed to be the emotional truth about the world we live in—and urge men and women to act out their teachings in appropriately simplistic and hostile ways.

The popular "good guy/bad guy" war story actually presents myths and beliefs about war that we have inherited from our ancestors. This modern myth pulls together many of the traditional motivations and explanations for war, and blends centuries of mythic ideas about revenge and glory, greediness and fear, pride and

rebellion, into a single plot. Despite the up-to-date technology and the special effects, the "good guy/bad guy"
plot—as well as the vision of the universe on which it
rests—is thousands of years old.

Myths and war have a great deal to do with each other.
Mythic thought provides an explanation and an excuse
for war, as well as the motivation to fight. Indeed, as
the leaders and thinkers of the major nations of the world
agreed in 1945, when UNESCO (United Nations Educational, Scientific, and Cultural Organization) was
founded, "wars begin in the minds of men."[2] In other
words, it is the emotions of men and women—translated into mythic stories and accepted as action-evoking
truths—that lead us to prepare for and fight wars.

The UNESCO charter goes on to say, "Since wars
begin in the minds of men, it is in the minds of men
that we have to erect the ramparts of peace." For those
defensive walls of peace to succeed, however, we must
diminish the emotional power of war. We must analyze
and criticize the myths of war because they give force
and direction to the engines of violence. Only when we
understand and consciously reject the "reasons" for war
can we hope to build cities of peace.

Chapter Two

The Puzzle of War

There is an old movie on television.

It is winter in high plains country, and a constant wind scatters powdery flakes from scant patches of snow. A small band of Indians, Ojibway warriors, moves silently and quickly. Huddled against the cold, they are following a barely visible trail toward a low ridge of hills.

The leader of the war party glances backward, then speaks to his men. "The Sioux are not far away," he tells them. "When we get to the hills, we will wait near the river, in ambush." He makes a gesture of contempt. "We will show them they cannot offend Ojibway honor!"

When at last the trail brings them to their destination, the leader speaks again.

"This is where we will ambush the Sioux."

He motions to one of the warriors and indicates a fallen tree. "Go," he commands. "Hide there."

The warrior immediately flattens his body against the cold ground, prepared to wait silently until the Sioux come.

The leader speaks again. "You. Go there."

Another man hides, not far from the first.

"Now you."

The next warrior hides. The leader continues, until all are hidden.

"No one fires until I give the command," the leader reminds them.

They wait in silence, until from the distance come sounds of a large party of Sioux. The group of enemy Sioux laugh and talk as they come along the trail, suspecting no danger. Closer and closer they come, as the Ojibway warriors, silent and eager, watch their leader.

People who create stories often put their own beliefs and ways of understanding things into the plots. Most writers would assume that Indian war leaders would think and act the way American and European generals have in similar situations.[1]

How *do* such generals think and act? One example occurred in 1708, when the Duke of Marlborough had charge of some British and Dutch forces. His men were near the French coast at a place called Wynendael. Their objective was to defeat French troops that had been assigned to protect the coastal territory.

Marlborough, like the Ojibway chief, hid his men on either side of a narrow valley through which the French soldiers had to pass. They waited until the French forces were all in the valley; then, when Marlborough gave a signal, his forces set upon the trapped men from all sides. Three thousand French troops were killed at Wynendael before the rest refused to continue fighting. And the Duke of Marlborough and the British were jubilant over this victory—even though they had lost a thousand of their own men in the battle.

If scriptwriters expected the Ojibway to think and act in the same way as Marlborough and other European and American generals, they would write a story in which the Ojibway sprang out of hiding and killed as many Sioux as possible.

And they would be wrong.

The incident between the Ojibway and the Sioux actually took place during the 1850s near present-day St. Paul, Minnesota, and the Ojibway did something quite different. The Ojibway stayed in hiding, waiting for their leader to give the signal to attack, while the long line of Sioux passed. Finally, one Sioux—for some reason a little slower than the rest—came alone.

When the Ojibway leader gave a signal, only one of his warriors fired. He grievously wounded the Sioux, who staggered and fell on his side. The Ojibway warrior rushed forward, catching him by the arm, and dragged him toward a clump of bushes.

As the wounded Sioux was being dragged along, he died.

"Cut his throat," the Ojibway leader shouted. "At once!"

Moving quickly, the warrior slit the Sioux's throat and, following ancient custom, cut away his scalp. Once he had done this, the entire group of Ojibway ran toward the river. They used a canoe that they had hidden there earlier and made their escape to the opposite shore.

Meanwhile, the sound of gunfire had attracted the attention of the Sioux. They hastened back, but were unable to overtake the Ojibway. They stood helplessly on the bank, watching the Ojibway dancing on the other shore, waving the bloody scalp and taunting them.

The Ojibway and the Sioux believed that it was right and necessary to make war, that their ancestors and their gods expected them to do so, but the Ojibway and the Sioux did not believe it was necessary to kill more than one man in order to achieve victory. Marlborough, however, had to kill thousands and suffer serious losses of his own men in order to satisfy his idea of a true war. How can such dissimilar ideas and actions all be called "war"?

What, exactly, is war?

A small child might define war as "a bunch of guys fighting." If asked to explain the difference between war and some other kinds of fighting the child would probably say that war is "a bunch of guys fighting with guns and planes and rockets and stuff." That's not a bad definition, as far as it goes. But there were wars before there were guns and rockets. Tribal people like the Ojibway and the Sioux had wars, and wars have been fought by knights on horseback and sailors in galleons. A good definition of war has to allow for all kinds of weapons. What's more, war is different from "just fighting" in some very basic ways.

In warfare there is always an objective. War is not just aggression or killing. These things happen in warfare, but they also happen at other times. War is a very specialized form of aggression and killing. It is organized by a tribe or a nation for a specific purpose: to take revenge, to conquer new lands, to defend against an enemy. The objectives of wars may be very different among different peoples, which is why it may be difficult to understand the actions of the Ojibway and the Sioux.

Whatever the objective for which a war is fought, it must be approved by the majority of people who go to war. First, the people must support the very idea of war. They must support both the preparations for it and the actual decision to fight.

A war requires a large investment of time, energy and resources even before it has begun. Ojibway men, for example, spent much time training to be warriors. They also had to make special weapons and special war clothes, and Ojibway women and girls had to prepare travel food to be carried by the warriors.

Similar preparations for war, even during a period of peace, occur in our own society. Though we are not at war, the United States spends over half the annual federal budget to support the military. We maintain a relatively small but well-trained army, navy and air force.

We stockpile thousands of nuclear warheads and keep them ready for instant firing. We commit the best minds among our scientists and engineers to developing bigger, better and faster weapons. And the Soviets and other countries do the same. Modern societies devote much time and energy to keeping their war systems ready for action.

Even with all these preparations, the decision to fight a war requires even more—a diversion of time, energy and goods. The Ojibway men who were part of the ambush party were not available to hunt or fish or work for their tribe. While the men were off fighting, the women had to take over some of the work that would otherwise be done by the men. Also, in addition to their own regular chores, they would go through rituals intended to bring success in battle to the men. Inevitably, the Ojibway produced fewer everyday goods while they were fighting—and their children ran the risk of losing their fathers.

Like the people of a tribe, the people of an industrialized nation must make sacrifices to support the decision to fight a war. The effort involved in fighting World War II, for example, required the establishment of a draft forcing all able-bodied young men to serve in the army until peace was achieved. Factories and shipyards that normally produced consumer goods had to be converted to the production of war supplies, and new factories had to be built to meet the needs of the military. In order to replace the men who were needed for combat duty, women volunteered to join military services like the

Women's Army Corps. They also took jobs in the factories and shipyards. Since many of these women had small children, the government quickly created and financed thousands of child-care centers.[2]

In order to pay for the military and its supplies, taxes were raised and civilians were urged to buy war bonds as a gesture of patriotism. To avoid inflation—civilian goods were in short supply and yet there was a great deal of spending money because almost everyone was working—the government established rationing of scarce goods and control of prices and wages.

While some of these drastic changes were enforced by the government, many—such as women's war work or buying war bonds—depended on the civilians' voluntary cooperation. And even government regulations like gas rationing or price control ultimately depended for their effectiveness on people's willingness to obey the law and sacrifice individual desires for the common good.

Sometimes during a long war, ordinary citizens decide that they can't trust their government. They come to believe—for one reason or another—that defeat is inevitable and further sacrifices are useless. When that happens, even the most autocratic government cannot continue to fight and must seek peace. Thus, if the majority of the people are not willing to support wars, wars cannot be fought.

This happened to Imperial Germany during World War I (1914–1918). In the early years of that war, the German people were very supportive of the war effort. They worked hard, fought bravely, and accepted many sacrifices of food and comfort as the price of helping their country. Neither they nor their representatives objected when the Kaiser created a military dictatorship, giving two generals, Ludendorff and Hindenburg, control over almost every aspect of German life.

In the autumn of 1918, however, the military dictators asked their enemies for an armistice. The generals did not believe they were as yet defeated; no foreign troops had yet occupied German soil and Germany still governed large areas of France and Russia. But their summer offensive in France had failed, and preparing a new one would be difficult. An armistice would give them a chance to negotiate—and to prepare for a later offensive if that should prove necessary.

The news that their leaders had sought an armistice came, however, as an enormous shock to the ordinary German civilians and soldiers. Until that moment they had been assured that Germany was on the verge of winning the war; now it seemed that they had been lied to (and they had). They lost trust in their leaders and became unwilling to bear the sacrifices that continued fighting would entail.

When the German government tried to reject the harsh conditions their enemies demanded for an armistice, and continue the war, the German people refused to obey their leaders. The imperial navy mutinied; workers in factories making weapons went on strike; masses of people demonstrated in the streets. The generals had to confess to the Kaiser that the troops were so discontented that they could not be used either to fight the enemy or to restore order at home. The Kaiser and his generals were powerless—and the war was over!

We now have the beginnings of a definition of war. We know that war is an organized form of aggression or killing with a specific goal, and that it must have the support of the tribe or nation. Wars have another important characteristic: They have always been primarily male enterprises.

Throughout history there have been exceptions. A few individual women have been soldiers, and queens— such as Isabella of Spain or Elizabeth I of England— have commanded armies. In very desperate situations women have helped to defend besieged cities or even been deliberately used on the battlefield. The Russians in World War II, for example, had female soldiers at the front, in combat, during the German invasion of their homeland. Similarly, revolutionary armies, attacking traditional ways of ordering society, have included women as combat soldiers. For example, women were active members of the informal combat units that fought to establish the state of Israel in the 1940s.[3]

Despite the fact that women are quite capable of fighting, most societies do not believe they should fight. Women are needed at home to be wives and mothers, many people argue. Others believe we should not train women to be fierce, because then they will not be suitable mothers. Some military men simply say that it's women they're fighting to protect.

Warfare, in fact, is thought to be a particularly masculine pursuit. Israeli generals, for example, learned in the wars of the late 1960s and early 1970s that it was unwise to put women in the front lines, but for a reason having nothing to do with their combat abilities. Whenever the Islamic soldiers who were fighting against Israel knew they were in combat with units that contained women, they fought with terrible desperation. These men would rather have died than surrender to an army that included females. The belief that it would be a disgrace to be defeated by women illustrates how much manhood and a capacity for battle have come to be regarded as almost the same thing by many people.

Women, nonetheless, are expected to support wars: to approve of the preparations for war, to work in the factories that make weapons, and even to serve in noncombat roles in the armies and navies of the world. Without women's approval and support, it would be very difficult—perhaps even impossible—to have a war.

If we put all these things we know about war together, we have a definition of war that can serve for any war, fought for any reason: *War is an organized action of aggression or defense, planned and prepared for in advance to achieve certain goals that have the approval of the tribe or nation. It is carried out primarily by men, but must be supported by women.*

Some people, realizing that wars have been fought throughout recorded history, argue that warfare is somehow built into human nature, that it is instinctive and therefore unavoidable. This is not true.

In this World War I poster, a charming young woman symbolizes the supporting roles women play in war. The Bettmann Archive, Inc.

An activity is instinctive only if it is behavior that is inherited at birth, encoded in the genes of the smallest infant. Much animal behavior is instinctive. Fish know how to swim at birth; most birds know how to fly; calves know how to walk. Even more complicated behavior patterns among animals, such as those involving hunting, courtship and raising young, are also often instinctive and do not have to be learned.[4]

Human babies, however, have a very different inheritance. They must learn to crawl and to walk, to talk and to use their hands effectively. In fact, only a few simple activities such as sucking, grasping and smiling seem to be determined by genetic coding. Instead, what seems to be instinctive to humans is the urge to learn and create culture.

Can people argue that war is instinctive because getting angry and fighting seem natural? People start hitting even when they are babies. We can all remember, at some time when we were young, being angry and hitting—or trying to hit—someone who was teasing us or took something away from us. And what about all the bickering and scrapping that go on between brothers and sisters?

Warfare is not the same thing as individual anger or individual fighting. Warfare certainly makes use of the human capacity for anger and aggressive action, but only in a very disciplined and controlled way.

While a decision to go to war may—or may not—be motivated by anger, the soldiers who actually fight may feel very little of that emotion. Indeed, during World

War I, troops often felt so little hostility toward each other that they had to be prohibited from "fraternizing"—in particular, from celebrating Christmas together in the barren wastes of "no-man's-land," the devastated and shell-cratered territory in France between the trenches of the two armies.

The usual mood of soldiers at the beginning of battle is not anger but a combination of excitement, fear and determination. Effective military action, in fact, would be almost impossible if it depended on angry soldiers: a really angry soldier may take inappropriate or rash actions, and therefore endanger the lives of others. This is why men have to be specially trained to be soldiers, rather than be allowed to do things—such as run away—that they might do if they followed their emotions.

When people enter military service, the first thing they have to do is go through basic training. Much of this training time is devoted to military discipline. Military trainees must learn, in particular, to respond immediately to orders. They are pushed to keep going when they are tired, and made to undertake difficult tasks when they are afraid. They are forced, again and again, to ignore or suppress their own individuality and individual desires. They do not instinctively know how to be soldiers.

Most men are also reluctant to kill other human beings. This is true even of men who have been well trained and believe passionately in their cause.

Research undertaken to increase military effectiveness has proved just how difficult it is to train men to kill.

During World War II, U.S. government researchers investigated how men behaved during battle. They found that fear of killing, rather than fear of being killed, was the most common reason men did not perform as well as they had been expected to.

The soldiers who fought in World War II had learned to use guns primarily on target ranges. The emphasis in their training with rifles had been on accuracy, on waiting until one could see the enemy clearly. They were taught that bullets must not be wasted on nonmoving targets, and so this kind of training stressed making ammunition count. Investigation showed, however, that only about 15 percent of the men trained in this manner fired—even once—in a battle.[5]

By the time of the Korean conflict, which began in 1950, a need was seen for new training methods. New training, with a different emphasis, was devised by S.L.A. Marshall, an army veteran and one of the researchers who had investigated the actions of soldiers during World War II. The goal of the new training was to overcome the soldiers' reluctance to fire their guns—to kill other humans. Soldiers were taught to fire on command, and to fire at nonhuman, nonmoving targets: the trees at the front of a woods, or perhaps some object at the crest of a hill.

This new training was effective. It more than tripled the proportion of men who actually fired during a battle— instead of 15 percent, as during World War II, it was 50 percent in Korea. But still, half the men did not fire.

Even with the most carefully designed training programs, soldiers are reluctant to kill.[6]

Moreover, most men have not been soldiers. This was true especially during the times of the great military empires, like those of Egypt or Rome, that have dominated much of history. In such empires, the rulers made war with special, full-time armies; ordinary people tried to go on with their daily lives.

Most kings and emperors deliberately did not draft their peasants or craftsmen into armies. They needed them instead for the crops and tools they produced and for the taxes they paid. During the sixteenth and seventeenth centuries in Japan, only a noble samurai warrior could legally own a sword or a gun. Most rulers weren't eager to have peasants trained as soldiers. Indeed, they feared that peasants, if given military skills and equipment, would rebel against the tax-collecting government and attempt to overthrow it.

Surely these peasants would have rebelled against the prohibition on owning weapons if the desire to make war were instinctive, a "natural" part of human nature.

War is not instinctive. But humans do create complex patterns of activity—as individuals or as groups. And they learn to repeat the activities that their societies value, whether it be playing the electric guitar, going to college or making war. But there is nothing predetermined about any of these activities.

Indeed, the earliest human beings apparently did not make war. Archaeologists have carefully studied evidence left behind by early societies, yet have unearthed no indications of war among people who lived during the long period when humans got all their food through hunting and gathering. Warfare did not occur until humans learned to grow crops and keep animals.[7]

One group of early humans who did not wage war were the Cro-Magnons, a surprisingly advanced people who lived more than thirty thousand years ago. The Cro-Magnon people left beautiful pictures of horses, bison, reindeer and mammoths on the walls of caves in central France. Animals are the main subjects of the pictures, but there are human forms too. The pictures were made by skilled artists, and we know the Cro-Magnon were also skilled at making flint tools, spearheads, needles and other useful objects.[8]

No one knows for certain why the Cro-Magnon made their pictures of animals, but the most logical guess is that the pictures were used during rites of magic intended to assure successful hunting. Similar rites are still used today by such hunting-and-gathering peoples as the Eskimos. During these rites the men act out a successful hunt, using symbols and pictures representing the animals they wish to kill.

We can be fairly certain the Cro-Magnon did not make magic to assure success in war, because we have found no pictures of battles or slain enemies. Also, archaeologists have found no distinctive war weapons among the thousands of remains left by the Cro-Magnon or any other very early human societies.

Weapons used to kill animals can, of course, also be used to kill human beings. But societies that wage war tend to distinguish between hunting and war-making weapons. Their war weapons may be designed differently, or they may be given unique decorations. The Ojibway, for example, made a special bow for use in war. It was decorated with carved, red-painted designs. These special, magical figures, the Ojibway believed, would increase the bow's strength and effectiveness. If the need to make war were instinctive, evidence of war weapons would be found in all human societies.

Most researchers agree that war and agriculture came into existence during the period when the Cro-Magnons began to disappear. This was about ten thousand years ago, at the beginning of Neolithic times. The word "neolithic" means "new stone," and it refers to the complex stone tools humans developed then. It also refers to agriculture. Neolithic people began planting crops and raising animals instead of relying on hunting and gathering to obtain their food.

Dwelling places of very early Neolithic farmers have been discovered in both the Near East and China. In most of these sites archaeologists have found remains of houses that were quite simple. But they have also found impressive mud or stone walls surrounding the villages. Such walls would have taken an enormous amount of time and energy to construct and maintain. Since wild animals can be more easily and cheaply repelled by the fire and weapons of villagers, such walls are a sign that the villagers feared a raid from another group of human beings. They are unmistakable evidence that humans had begun to engage in wars.[9]

We have much evidence that warfare is not instinctive, yet some people still argue that we cannot avoid war. After all, such people say, wars have been fought by humans—century after century—for thousands of years. What can be done to change patterns of thought and action that go back beyond the beginnings of written history?

This attitude ignores the fact that humans have in the past made radical changes in their cultures; that we have already abandoned institutions—like slavery or the legal and political inferiority of women—that were also thousands of years old. For example, slavery as a human institution is almost as old as war. The Egyptians and the Babylonians, the Greeks and the Romans—all major civilizations—took slavery for granted. People believed that it was either divinely ordained by the gods or determined by the natural inferiority of some human beings. (The Greek philosopher Aristotle, for example, believed that slaves, as individuals, were naturally slavish.) When the United States was founded, large numbers of human beings—mostly black and mostly in the Southern states—were slaves, and their enslavement was justified by references to the Bible and to the supposed natural inferiority of the black race. At the same time, however, white slaves worked the coal mines in Scotland—and earlier pulled the oars of the great triremes of the French, Spanish and Ottoman navies.

Starting in the late eighteenth century, however, a small group of men and women began to deny the ideas on which slavery was based, insisting instead that both the Bible and natural law taught the equality and inherent liberty of all human beings. Slowly but persistently they converted others to their beliefs. It was a difficult political task because they were, after all, threatening an accepted form of ownership of property. They were able to pass laws that outlawed, first, the trade in slaves and eventually slavery itself.

Today all members of the United Nations formally agree that slavery is a violation of human rights—and the institution has almost vanished from human societies. Even where it exists—as it is reported to in small numbers in some underdeveloped and autocratic countries—it is considered embarrassing and tends to be hidden from foreign observation.

Change begins with understanding. While there are many things to understand about war, one very important idea to remember is this: *A war cannot be carried out effectively without the people's approval and support.*

This is true even in a dictatorship. Of course, in an autocracy the people cannot influence government policy as immediately and easily as in a democracy. But people's passive consent is important to a dictatorship, even in peacetime; that is why dictators rely on attractive propaganda as well as powerful secret police to bolster their regimes. Effective war-making, however, requires more than passive acceptance. It needs the active cooperation of the entire public. Moreover, even the strongest dictator lacks the resources necessary to both make war and coerce his own people at the same time.

Stalin, for example, had to abandon his hostility to religion during World War II in order to make his government seem worth fighting and dying for. Even so, many of the minority populations under Soviet control, such as the Ukrainians, hoped for a better life under the Germans. They initially welcomed their German conquerors with open arms, seriously hampering Russian resistance. Only after they had experienced the brutal, racist policy of the Germans did most Ukrainians become willing to actively cooperate with the Soviet government as the lesser of two evils. (Indeed, it seems likely that the current Soviet leadership is encouraged to be peaceful at least in part by a realistic fear of what might happen in Eastern Europe and some of the non-Russian Soviet states in any future major war!)

The need for the people's approval and consent is true even for a nuclear war. We tend to think that such a war is different, because the decision to "push the button" would have to be made so quickly that people would not have a chance to make their wishes known. However, the weapons that make such a war possible must first be built and maintained and newer, more powerful weapons constantly designed and put in place. This cannot be done without the consent of the people, even if this consent is passive and occurs simply because nobody objects. If enough citizens actively refuse their consent, governments can be blocked from continuing to amass weapons of ultimate destruction.

Wars are not part of human nature; furthermore, they require the consent of the people of a tribe or of a nation. As surely as war is not instinctive, it is not inevitable.

Chapter Three

Revenge and Magic

If war is not instinctive, why did our early farming ancestors decide that such a costly and destructive activity was necessary? What good did they think they accomplished by battle? And why were primitive warriors like the Ojibway satisfied when they killed only a single member of the enemy tribe?

The task of investigating the earliest forms of warfare has been a difficult one. Our remote ancestors left only certain kinds of evidence of the way they lived: tools, the walls of their homes or villages, burial remains and even paintings—but no written records. Archaeologists and historians know in very general terms what people did, but not why.

However, we can gain some understanding of our

ancestors' motivation by turning to studies anthropologists have made of farming tribes—like the Ojibway—whose way of life remained similar to that of Neolithic people until very recently. We know how they fought—and how they explained their need to wage war. As a result, we know that these neolithic people went to war as part of a magic ritual for maintaining control of their world.

Human beings have been making magic for a very long time. Our earliest ancestors lived in a world without scientific knowledge. They did not understand ice and fire, winter and summer, rain and drought. Yet, as a species, humans seem to need to understand and control their world. In order to avoid the terrifying feeling that they lived in an out-of-control situation in which they could take no action to obtain the things they wanted or needed, early humans created magic rituals. They made magic to bring rain, to cure the sick, to make the hunt successful, to ensure good harvests. Indeed, such rituals were already old when the Cro-Magnons painted the caves in southern France as a form of magic to assure successful hunts.[1]

For neolithic people, warfare was part of religion. Battle was simply one part of the most costly and potent of their magic rites. They believed warfare took place under the leadership and protection of sacred ancestral forces and that warfare was necessary to keep the universe in order. War ceremonies, therefore, were carried out carefully; complicated rules and taboos determined what people must or must not do. Once we understand battle as magic, much that seems puzzling—the action of the Ojibway, for example—becomes clear.

The war ceremonies of neolithic tribes varied, but neolithic warfare itself followed a basic pattern. The first step was always a ceremony believed to call the spirits of the dead into action and to give the warriors special powers.

The magic of war began with traditional songs and dances, during which the dead ancestors of the tribe were asked for help. The sacred "fighting stones" or "war bundles," which contained special ancestral or spirit powers, were brought out of their "resting" place. In order to be even closer to the spirits of their dead ancestors, the warriors decorated their bodies and wore special clothes.

Throughout the time of war, when men were associating themselves with the powers of Death, they followed rules that prohibited them from associating with women. By neolithic understanding, men could take on the power of Death, but women were naturally endowed with Life. Women were thought to possess special powers connected with their capacity to give birth. Neolithic people believed it would be dangerous to mix the powers of Death and Life.[2]

Although women were kept separate from men during a war ritual, they usually had their own rituals, which were considered equally necessary for success in battle. For example, when the ferocious Zulu men of Africa were away at war, their wives were not to quarrel or wear any ornaments. If they did, the Zulus feared, the men would suffer evil consequences. Instead, the women painted their faces in a special way, worked only in the very early hours of the morning and spent the rest of the day beating special large stones together and rattling smaller ones. The Zulu women believed these activities had a magic power that would keep death from their husbands.[3]

These customs may seem strange and illogical to us, but, in fact, the first steps in a neolithic war ritual were similar to things done by modern men and women. We also put our soldiers in special uniforms and keep our women away from the battlefield. We wave flags, hold big parades and sing special patriotic songs as we prepare to send men off to fight. We also remember the heroic success of our ancestors; our ministers, priests and rabbis assure us that God is on our side. We do these things primarily for psychological reasons: We know they will evoke a fighting spirit among our men and make it easier for people to bear their losses.

Fighting was the second major step in the magic ceremony of neolithic warfare. The fighting might have been a face-to-face encounter to which the enemy had been invited, or an ambush-type raid such as that staged by the Ojibway. In either case, it would have been very different from a modern battle.

In an ambush, the attacking warriors might have sought

The neolithic war rituals of the Dani tribe in New Guinea provide valuable insights into our own past. (following pages)
The Film Study Center, Harvard University; Karl G. Heider

to kill only one person, or they might kill several of the enemy. Since even the death of a small child was a source of powerful magic, the warriors were permitted to kill women or children as well as grown men. If both sides had decided upon war, the men might have agreed to meet for face-to-face fighting at a place where such battles were traditionally fought. This type of battle could last for several days, but would have been interrupted each day at sundown.

Despite their belief in the power brought about by killing, neolithic tribes tended to have rules that limited the amount and deadliness of fighting. There would have been restrictions on what the warriors could eat or drink, and on what kind of weapons they used. Some tribes, for instance, used feathers to make their hunting arrows fly with great accuracy, but would not use feathers on their war arrows. Other tribes required warriors to eat a hotly seasoned stew when they were preparing for battle, but forbade them to drink water until the battle had stopped. (As they got thirsty, they would increasingly become ready to call it quits.)

These limits on the damage inflicted by battles were very important. Enemies were necessary; magical control could be maintained only by regularly engaging in warfare. Because "enemy" tribes were really partners, they could not be annihilated. The tribes needed each other.

Except in quite unusual circumstances, one or two deaths would end a battle or an ambush. The tribe that suffered a death—after they held traditional mourning rites—would begin planning another round of warfare in order that they too might successfully complete the magic ritual.

The tribe that had inflicted a death, however, would begin the last step in the ritual of war. This involved special procedures and celebrations to assure prosperity and renewal of life for their people. The power the warriors had acquired by killing an enemy had to be transformed into a source of increased prosperity and fertility for the tribe.

Particular responsibilities fell on the warrior who had killed during battle. He would gain great prestige and praise for his action, but he would also be feared. He was thought to be powerful and dangerous, and so had to be kept away from the village until he had been purified. During his short exile, he would associate only with other men who had previously killed in battle. Usually the warrior would seek to experience a special vision or song that would give him increased, but safe, power in the future.

While the warriors who had killed an enemy were changing their personal power into controlled and usable forms, the rest of the people celebrated. If the body of a slain enemy had been captured, it might be gloated over, or even eaten. The skull, head or scalp would become magic objects to be used in future rituals.[4]

Because neolithic tribes associated women with new life, it was typically women—not warriors—who played the major role in this final part of the war ritual. The South American Jivaro, famed as headhunters, gave the shrunken heads of slain enemies to the women of the warriors' families. Ojibway women carried the scalp poles and led the dances that celebrated the victory. Now the women and their children would live, and live well![5]

When the people of a neolithic tribe had successfully concluded a war ritual, they felt they had assured their continued prosperity and fertility. They had completed a magic act, which they believed gave them power and control over an uncertain and hostile world.

We tend to feel superior to such "primitive" tribes and their belief in magic. Nonetheless, neolithic war had certain admirable qualities. Because of the limits that neolithic people placed on the murderous aspects of war and because of their willingness and ability to abide by rules to limit its deadliness, such wars were much less costly than battles fought in recent times.

Moreover, neolithic people seemed to have a clearer understanding than we do of the psychological aspects of battle. They understood that a warrior who kills another human being is affected emotionally by the experience, and they provided a ritual by which men who have killed could come to terms with what they had done and learn to use the experience creatively. Throughout much of modern history, men returning from battle also have been greeted with celebrations and reassured that their actions benefited their people. But the United States in the 1960s and early 1970s sent men into battle in Vietnam without providing them with a ritual to help them return to civilian life. Instead of being welcomed as heroes with parades and speeches, Vietnam veterans were shunned by civilians who blamed them for the war or, ironically, the failure of the war. As a result, many of these men, who risked their lives for their country, have continued to suffer emotionally from their wartime experiences. And some have expressed their suffering with acts of violence and despair—sniper killings, cruelty to their families or suicide.[6]

Moreover, we are not as far advanced from the magic of the neolithic people as we would like to think. Some people half seriously believe in magic. They choose special numbers for lottery tickets, carry lucky charms or avoid black cats. And we have inherited a far more consequential remainder of neolithic belief: Many people still harbor a deep-down feeling that warfare makes things right again. This is one of the feelings underlying the plot structure of the "good guy/bad guy" myth. In a sense, we do believe—as did neolithic people—that warfare can restore order to an out-of-control world.

When the Ayatollah Khomeini reminded the Iranian people in 1983 that war was a "surgical operation commanded by God the all-powerful,"[7] he clearly demonstrated a continuation of neolithic faith in war as an essential religious ritual. Even when we use more rational-sounding phrases, we are giving credibility to belief in the magic of war. The United States fought World War I because people were convinced it would "end all wars." Similarly, World War II was fought to "make the world safe for democracy." In both cases, we were seeking to invoke the magic of the war ritual to ensure prosperity and happiness.

Our understanding of what neolithic people thought was accomplished through the ritual of war—and of the traits we share with them—raises another very important question. *Why* did humans invent the special, hostile magic of war when they became farmers?

How do neolithic people like the Ojibway, the Zulus or the Jivaro explain their addiction to warfare? A warrior of such a tribe, if asked about the reasons his people so often go to war, would probably first say it was for revenge. He would say his tribe had been injured; that it wanted to avenge that injury by inflicting harm on the enemy tribe. This is not hard to understand. Each of us has, at some time, wanted to get back at somebody who caused us pain or embarrassment.

But what about a battle that was not connected with a death or injury caused by deliberate human action? Suppose the tribe had decided to fight as the result of a random, accidental event: a falling rock, the illness of a prized animal, unusual weather or even a special dream-vision. How can revenge make any sense in such situations?

Children who are very young and have less understanding of their world often feel singled out for misfortune and want to blame someone or something for the disaster. They may say that a tricycle tipped them over and "made" them skin a knee—and even seek to "punish" the tricycle by kicking it. In the same way, the neolithic warrior would explain that nothing is simply an accident; everything is deliberate or "caused." Someone or some spirit is always to blame.

Such a warrior would go on to answer that taking vengeance is always required in response to an injury. It's not a matter of whether anyone in the tribe personally feels angry or not; the dead require vengeance. If the living don't seek revenge, their dead ancestors will be angry. Angry ancestors can bring misfortune, he will say. They will stop protecting and helping the tribe, and may even seek to harm unworthy, ungrateful descendants.

If a neolithic warrior is asked how he knows that the dead require vengeance, he will tell a story. It will be a creation myth, a story about the beginning of his tribe's existence. Specifically, the story will tell how a heroic or divine person began the tribe's ritual of warfare.

For example, the Yanomamo, a constantly warring tribe of farmers who live in the Amazon jungles of Brazil, describe themselves as "the fierce people." A Yanomamo warrior will explain why his tribe fights so much by saying that in the beginning of time there were only the original beings. These beings created most of the important plants, animals and other things, but then most of them died in a great flood. Periboriwa, the spirit of the moon—an evil being—was one of the few who remained.

After the flood, according to the Yanomamo creation myth, the evil Periboriwa began to come down to the earth to eat the soul part of children. On Periboriwa's first descent, he ate a child, placing the child's soul between two pieces of cassava bread. He came a second time to eat another child, also with cassava bread. On

Periboriwa's third trip, two brothers named Uhdima and Suhirina became angry and decided to shoot him. Uhdima let his arrow fly, but he missed. Then Suhirina took one special bamboo-tipped arrow and shot at Periboriwa when he was directly overhead.

Suhirina's bamboo-tipped arrow hit Periboriwa in the stomach, and although the tip of the arrow barely went in, the wound bled greatly. Periboriwa fled back into the sky, but his blood spilled to earth, changing into men and causing many people to be born. And that, the Yanomamo explain, is why they are so fierce. Their tribe—and warfare—had its origins in the blood of Periboriwa.[8]

The Chiricahua Apaches of the American Southwest have a similar myth. In the beginning, they say, humans shared the earth with animals, monsters and certain heroic figures. Two of these heroic beings were White Painted Woman and her son Child of Water. Unfortunately, both White Painted Woman and human beings were regularly preyed upon by a monster, Giant. Indeed, Giant had eaten several of White Painted Woman's other children.

One day Child of Water and his brother Killer of Enemies were out hunting, and they met Giant. Child of Water knew how Giant had hurt his mother, so he decided to kill him, and after a great many tries, he was successful. Child of Water then proceeded to conquer the other monsters, such as Giant Eagle and Dangerous Buffalo. He didn't kill the eagle and the buffalo, however. Instead, he forced them to agree to serve human beings in the future.

Then, just before he and his mother departed for their home in the sky, Child of Water taught the Apaches all the proper magic rituals they would need. (During a war ritual, all Apache warriors are called Child of Water, and all Apache women White Painted Woman.)[9]

There is a basic pattern to the creation myths of the Yanomamo and the Apaches, and the creation myths of all war-making neolithic tribes share this pattern. It always has four steps.

First, there is an original time when things were good and all creatures were happy. Second, a new and murderous force appears, or one of the initially good forces becomes evil and destructive; the world becomes chaotic and there is much unhappiness. Third, a hero emerges who overcomes the force that is causing destruction and chaos, killing or severely injuring the evil being. And, finally, all creation myths conclude with the beginning of a way of life for the tribe—a way of life that has since remained unchanged. The way of life established by the creation hero always requires warfare as a way of reinforcing the original destruction of evil.

Both the plot structure and the emotional content of creation myths are similar to our familiar "good guy/ bad guy" plot. There is a specific and definable evil that keeps good people from being happy. And this evil force can be overcome through an act of heroic violence.

It's one way of understanding the world, but not the

only way. For example, hunters and gatherers also recognize that humans suffer losses and sorrows, but they
do not share the neolithic belief that the forces of death
and destruction are a constant threat that must be battled.
On the contrary, their beliefs tend to emphasize the
essential goodness of the world. Grief, rather than anger,
is their usual response to misfortune.

The Pygmies of southern Africa, for example, believe
that they are the children of the Forest, which cares for
them and loves them. When something happens to the
Pygmies, when a beloved person dies or there is a drought,
they do not blame it on an evil spirit and think the Forest
is angry and wants to be avenged. Instead, they assume
the Forest is sad and needs to be cheered up. The Pygmies hold a special grieving-and-healing ceremony every
evening for several weeks. Accompanied by a sacred
flute, they sing to the Forest. (They are singing as well,
of course, to one another.) Soon, quite naturally, both
the Forest and the Pygmies will be feeling better.[10]

Certainly, hunters and gatherers have, as *individuals*,
wanted revenge, but *as a group* they don't glorify the
taking of vengeance. Instead, most hunting-and-gathering people try to minimize violent expressions of anger.
They feel it threatens their way of life.

Hunting-and-gathering tribes have created some interesting rituals for expressing angry feelings. Unlike
war rituals, these are not costly to the tribe. Eskimos,
for example, have cursing festivals, during which angry
feelings are harmlessly spent, transformed into the creative use of language. But unlike the neolithic farmers,

the Eskimos don't believe that any magic power is acquired through this ceremony.[11]

Neolithic farmers are very different, in temperament and beliefs, from the gentle people who lead a hunting-and-gathering life. Neolithic people experience strong feelings of anger and resentment. They see the world as a dangerous, frightening place. These new and widely shared emotions have been expressed in the myths about the origins of war and then acted out in the repetitive ritual of battle. Moreover, the source of these feelings is probably to be found in the changed nature of life and child rearing required by the shift to agriculture.

The invention of farming, like the discovery of fire and the invention of the wheel, was in many ways a step forward. Land that was farmed provided more food, and more predictably, than did natural, untended land. Farmers, unlike hunters and gatherers, did not constantly need to move around to find a food supply, and so they could more easily store food for winter months and for periods of scarcity. In a farming society, with its more plentiful food, more of the children who were born would survive to adulthood; the tribe would increase.

The development of agriculture brought many benefits, but there were also social and psychological costs. In particular, farmers lost the clear connection—characteristic of a hunting-and-gathering way of life—between what a person does and how soon he or she eats.

In a hunting-and-gathering tribe, women collect most of the food: nuts, berries, roots and other vegetables.

This takes perhaps half a day or less, according to what is in season and how hungry their families are. Men do the hunting of big animals, and apparently decide to do so whenever the idea of eating meat becomes tempting. They will be intensively busy for several days, engaged in a great adventure, after which there will be a tasty feast and a celebration of their success. Then they will rest for a week or two.

Most of the time, both men and women do things they want to do. They spend affectionate hours story-telling or singing, playing with children, making toys or just lying in the sun or by the fireside. Indeed, the anthropologist Marshall Shalins has called hunters and gatherers "an affluent people," not because they have many possessions, but because they have a great deal of free time.[12]

For both men and women, the work of getting food is directly motivated by hunger and promptly followed by the satisfaction of eating. As a result, hunting-and-gathering parents assume that their children, as adults, will also collect food or build huts whenever hunger or cold make such activities seem immediately desirable. They do not have to teach their children how to "work." Though the children need to learn complex skills and have much knowledge, their parents rely, successfully, on the natural desire of children to learn and to be considered "grown-ups."

Farming, on the other hand, requires a very different kind of life and takes a great deal of time and energy.

Land must be cleared, fences must be built to control animals, seeds must be planted, weeds must be pulled and plants must have water. Finally, the crops must be harvested and stored. A neolithic farmer is affluent with things, but not with leisure. He spends much more time working than does a hunter and gatherer.

What's more, farming chores are seldom immediately rewarding. Well over a year may pass from the time a jungle is cleared until the first crop of sweet potatoes or rice is harvested. And work times are dictated not by human desire but by the requirements of crops and the changes of season. With farming, the immediate connection between desire, activity and reward has been lost.

Why didn't farmers go back to a more leisurely way of life? Some probably did, and some groups of people may have switched back and forth for a time. But if a tribe stayed with farming for several generations, its size would increase. More people would have to get their living from the same land, and untended land could no longer support the whole tribe.

Farming could not be disinvented. The leisurely life of the hunter-gatherer was lost; the tasks of farming had become a necessity. Survival of the group required that adults work on a regular basis whether they felt like it or not.

Farming allowed humans to have some control over their world; but in order to exercise it, they had to control themselves. And they also had to teach their children to work whether they wanted to do so or not. There was, therefore, an enormous change in the way children were raised.

We see this in neolithic tribes that survive today. Beginning when they are very young, children of such farming tribes must help tend gardens and animals. Children of only five or six take care of younger brothers and sisters while their parents work. At around seven or eight, they are given responsibility for guarding pigs or acting as scarecrows. By ten or eleven, they will be responsible for weeding, harvesting and other tasks.

Parents in primitive farming tribes forcefully demand that children do all these chores, and punish refusal or inattention. They scold or shame their children for laziness—in front of all the other children and adults. And spankings, sometimes even beatings, are used regularly.[13]

Do these parents love their children less than hunting-and-gathering parents? No. They just want them to be successful, productive adults. Farming children must learn to take their obligations seriously and do what is needed regardless of how they feel at the moment.

Not surprisingly, this change in the way children are treated produces adults who are emotionally very different from hunting-and-gathering adults. They have what we might call a "neolithic personality."

The resentment so characteristic of neolithic warfare begins with children who feel resentful toward their parents. But their parents do not allow them to express this feeling and so get rid of it. Since the children love their parents and are dependent on them, they must repress their anger and resentment.

Unacknowledged feelings of shame are also important in a neolithic personality. Sometimes, when neolithic children have been scolded for not working hard enough or for expressing resentment, they may feel they do not deserve their parents' love. But feeling ashamed is unpleasant; children want to feel they do deserve their parents' approval. So children try to deny—even to themselves—their feelings of resentment and shame. They want to believe that they are always good and loving.

When these children grow up and themselves become parents, their feelings of resentment and shame—though buried—are still part of their characters. Their own parents, who have probably died, no longer tell them what to do, but they are still ruled by the customs of the tribe—the rules of their dead parents and all the other ancestors.

To a neolithic person, the world of spirits and ancestors is very real. Spirits are powerful, just as parents are powerful. People work hard to "be good" for their ancestors, and feel that it is not safe to resent or disobey them. And they expect the ancestors, being older and more powerful, to take care of them.

At the same time, they still harbor unconscious feelings of shame, and of resentment toward these ancestors. They fear the ancestors will find them unworthy and punish them. The idea that the world is a hostile and threatening place comes from inside neolithic people, from their own childhood and the treatment they experienced while they were growing up.[14]

When a neolithic tribe has problems—the harvest is poor or a healthy person becomes sick—the members of the tribe believe their world is angry. Bad events have causes; whatever caused the anger of the spirits or the ancestors must be discovered and remedied.

Who deserves to be punished? Has anyone in the tribe done something that merits punishment? Unless someone's misbehavior has been very obvious, the members of a tribe will not want to admit they have acted incorrectly. Especially, they do not want to consider whether anyone should be singled out as having feelings of resentment toward parents or the ancestors. Instead, blame is usually placed outside the tribe—on an evil spirit or on another tribe.

Shifting blame away from oneself or from one's group is a very common human response. Almost everyone does it. When students don't do their homework, they often avoid blaming themselves directly. "The movie on television just got too interesting," they might say. Or, "Is it my fault that all my friends picked that night to call on the phone?"

When a shifting of blame is done deliberately or consciously, it's called lying. But when it happens unconsciously—when people lie to themselves—psychologists call it "projection." It happens often. In particular, we project onto others qualities we don't want to acknowledge in ourselves. We may want to ignore or deny that we sometimes want to be lazy or to cheat. But we're aware that such emotions are present in our feelings, and so we may project them onto others—the poor or welfare recipients. (This also allows us to ignore the ways in which we, as part of the greater society, have failed such people.) Projection is an unconscious way of seeing ourselves in a good light, and of displacing blame onto others. Another person, or another group of people, may then be seen as less worthy, perhaps even immoral.

Of course, projection never represents the world as it really is. No one individual or group of individuals is totally good or totally bad—even though this is one of the messages in our modern "good guy/bad guy" myth. But projections can make us, at least temporarily, feel good about ourselves.

With neolithic tribes, projection is often a mutual affair. The Papago Indians believed that all Apaches were powerful and evil magicians; the Apaches had similar beliefs about the Papagos. The two tribes were unknowing partners, engaged in a game of mutual name-calling and denigration.

When people strongly dislike the qualities in themselves that they project onto others, they can become very hostile and destructive. Adolf Hitler engaged in projection at an extreme level of destructive intensity. He told the German people they were intelligent, hard-working, loyal and brave; Jews and other groups were labeled stupid, lazy, crafty and cowardly. German problems, Hitler declared, would be solved and the world made a better place if these people were exterminated.

Over six million Jews died in concentration camps and gas chambers because of the power of Hitler's hostile projections.[15]

When a neolithic tribe has blamed an outsider for something, it feels the wrongdoing must be punished in the same way children are punished: by violence. According to the creation myths, order can be restored only through violent acts. When the wrongdoer is punished, the ancestors will be pleased. And the members of the tribe will also be reassured that they are, indeed, "good," worthy individuals.

In most neolithic tribes, warfare was unquestioned. Once the mechanisms of war—the shared emotions, myths and rituals—were set up, they continued to function almost like an engine. Any battle was likely to produce a death; each death needed to be avenged. And if one cylinder of the war engine missed a stroke—if a battle did not produce a death—any random misfortune could serve as a spark to get the engine going again. Neolithic war was waged, therefore, in a repetitive and seemingly unending cycle.

But neolithic war was not inevitable. Not all agricultural tribes created the ritual of war. The Hopi, for example, lived in the same part of the American Southwest as the Apaches and also supported themselves by growing corn and maize. Yet they did not make war, either as a defensive measure or as a means of controlling their environment.

Geoffrey Gorer, an anthropologist, has pointed out that such peaceful societies all share certain traits. "They

all manifest enormous gusto for concrete physical pleasures—eating, drinking, sex, laughter. . . . Their religious life lacks significant personalized gods and devils;
a happy, hardworking and productive life is within the
reach of all."[16] In effect, they possess many of the cultural
and psychological features that are characteristic of hunting-and-gathering people. While they have to work hard,
their culture emphasizes the pleasurable aspects of life
and attempts to minimize individual resentment and guilt.

We do not know why, or how, the Hopi developed
a different culture and personality. In the absence of
written records, we cannot re-create their past. The Hopi
creation legends, however—which tell of three previous
worlds, each destroyed because humans forgot their sol-
idarity with creation and took to warfare and destruction—suggest that their present culture and personality
was not just simply and innocently inherited from their
preagricultural past.

Moreover, humans who created governments and
empires slowly abandoned the neolithic belief in battle
as a magic ritual and a proper outlet for revenge. Instead,
they channeled resentment primarily into courts of law.
Punishment became part of a judicial ritual.

Unfortunately, however, neither the psychological
habit of projection nor warfare itself has been abandoned. Encouraged by our modern myths about war,
we still project onto the stranger or the enemy the qualities we dislike and want to deny in ourselves. And—
though in different ways and for different objectives—
wars continue to be fought.

Chapter Four

Wars of Greed
and How They Began

In the early days of autumn, 331 B.C., a young Mace-
donian king stood with his army on the low foothills
of the Zagros mountains not far from the great city of
Babylon. This king was Alexander, later to be known
as Alexander the Great.[1]

From his homeland in the north of Greece, Alexander
had brought with him to this eastern land an army of
47,000 men. Alexander's father had spent almost all his
reign collecting and training these men, a professional
army of full-time soldiers. Alexander had inherited them
five years earlier, when his father was assassinated.

Below, on the broad plains that extended down to the
swift-flowing Tigris River, Alexander could see the armies
of his Persian enemy, the Emperor Darius. And despite
the large size of Alexander's army, his forces were greatly

outnumbered by the armies of Darius, which extended for miles on the plains below. The Persian multitude, as befitted an empire large and old, was much more diverse than Alexander's. Historians believe Darius's army must have numbered between 100,000 and 200,000 men.

Alexander, at this time just twenty-five years old, knew he must act quickly to plan his battle strategy. With a few of his companions, young noblemen who had been his friends since boyhood, Alexander rode out to see what could be learned. As Alexander and his friends studied Darius's huge army, they could identify—by their armor and costumes—units of Indians, Bactrians, Scythians and Persians. And they observed that the Emperor Darius had chosen a broad, flat battlefield. Even now his men were at work placing stakes and traps on the ground in front of the Persian line of defense, to make a frontal charge difficult for Alexander's army. Darius had obviously chosen a defensive strategy, which was only appropriate for a man defending territory he already ruled.

The center of the Persian emperor's camp had been given over to elephants from India, fearsome beasts. Horses could never be made to charge at them, or even go near them. And behind the elephants stood chariots, many with sharp scythes attached to their sides and wheels, defenses deadly to anyone foolish enough to come close when the chariots were in motion. Far beyond the chariots, spread out both to the left and the right, were the ponies of Darius's fierce cavalry. Their riders, nomads from the steppes, were superbly skilled.

Behind the chariots were many tents. The largest, with its gold ornaments and fluttering pennants, clearly belonged to Darius himself. Darius, Alexander knew, would follow tradition in tomorrow's battle and lead the chariots in person.

That afternoon Alexander collected his generals to make detailed plans. And then he put a great amount of time and energy into going from unit to unit in his encampment, speaking to his troops. Victory would be theirs, he told his men. And because he guessed that the army of Darius would stand at attention all night watching for a surprise attack, he instructed his men to sleep.

The next morning Alexander positioned highly trained infantrymen at the center of the battle line. They were armed with sarissas, sixteen-foot spears made of tough wood, each topped with an iron pike, weapons so heavy that it took two hands to hold them. When carried by ten rows of men and rapidly moved up and down, the sarissas projected a bristling wall of spears. Alexander knew it would make a startling sight, rather like a gigantic menacing porcupine moving across the battlefield.

On the left wing of his battle line, Alexander put horsemen from Thessaly, drawn up in diamond formations. On the right were his mounted scouts, carrying long spears. Scattered everywhere were men from Crete who were expert archers. And at the rear Alexander put scimitar-wielding Thracians, less disciplined but able to provide a fierce defense if the Persian troops managed to encircle Alexander's army and attack from behind.

Alexander himself would ride after the mounted scouts, leading his personal group of horsemen—the Royal Guard. Trained to follow their leader with astonishing speed, they always rode and fought in a wedge formation. They moved together as one person, and could make rapid feints to either side—or charge directly into and split open the enemy's line.

This battle was crucial for Alexander. He had earlier pushed the Persians back out of the area now known as Turkey, conquered the seaports of the Near East and then taken over Egypt, a rich old empire grown restless under Persian rule. But now Alexander was far from home. He could not afford a defeat. If he lost this battle, he might lose not only his newly won territories but his entire army and his power to rule his homeland as well.

Alexander knew that Darius was depending on the sheer power and numbers of his imperial forces to give him victory. Alexander would have to depend on skill and daring—and also on his memory and understanding of what kind of man Darius was.

When Alexander had fought Darius two years earlier, Darius had lost his nerve and fled from the battlefield. Alexander counted on his doing the same thing again, and so deliberately built his strategy around this possibility. It was a risk, but he was counting on the skill and toughness of his troops to make this gamble succeed.

Alexander opened the battle by leading his horsemen

A Roman mosaic depicting Alexander on his horse in a confrontation with Darius on his chariot during the battle at Issos—an earlier battle from which Darius fled. (following pages)   The Bettmann Archive, Inc.

in a charge far to the right, drawing the Persians after him. Encirclement—the seeming objective of Alexander's opening move—was a goal any military commander might hope to achieve. Once encircled, any army lost mobility and freedom; it could be slowly diminished until at last it surrendered.

The Persian commanders were not worried, however. The Persian army was so much greater in numbers, Alexander's forces could never succeed in encircling them. Encirclement was a much more appropriate tactic for Darius's army to use. Indeed, on the other side of the battlefield, the Persian forces were already starting their encircling move. Alexander's troops were being spread thin as they tried to contain the Persians.

As horses and men galloped and struggled in combat, a blinding dust rose from the dry plain. The gleaming flashes from the armor, brilliant in the early-morning sunlight, were softened in the dust clouds. Visibility diminished wherever men rode or fought. Troops on both sides, waiting restlessly to join the fight, found it increasingly difficult to make out what was happening.

Suddenly, however, from the dust cloud on the right emerged a distinctive figure: Alexander in his famous armor and helmet, followed by the Royal Guard. Leaving the mounted scouts to struggle as best they could against the increasing opposition of the Persians, Alexander and the Guards charged boldly toward the center of the Persian army. Riding at a diagonal, they galloped behind the stakes the Persians had set out, and then behind the elephants. They rode fearlessly on, directly into the cavalry and chariots surrounding Darius.

Troops at the center of the Persian line, waiting to move forward once the Macedonians had been encircled, were shocked by Alexander's sudden appearance. In their attempt to change fronts quickly, to turn and face the enemy that had so surprisingly appeared at their side, Darius's troops became entangled and confused. They were unable to effectively resist even so small a force as the men accompanying Alexander.

The Persian emperor, suddenly threatened with either death or capture, turned and fled. As the Persian Imperial Guard followed him, they unwittingly left undefended the center of their own rear line. Moreover, as word that the emperor had fled flew across the Persian lines, some troops faltered and still others found it wise to join the flight to the rear.

Alexander's gamble, his hope that Darius would again lose his nerve, had paid off. The compact Persian army had been broken into several pieces; it was now manageable by Alexander's smaller force. As Darius fled toward the Kurdish mountains in the northernmost reaches of his empire, Alexander stayed on the dusty battlefield. His men still had to overcome the remaining Persian forces, and their victory would not be secure until nightfall. Not until the next day would Alexander lead his men away, leaving behind the barren plain of battle and the thousands of rotting bodies on it.

This is a very different battle from that carried out by the Ojibway! Alexander's men—and Darius's too—were fighting at enormous distances from their homes. Not all their fighters used the same weapons and techniques. These armies were made up of special forces, such as infantry and cavalry. Each unit possessed its own special weaponry. Moreover, no single death was going to bring the battle to a conclusion; indeed, death as such was not the objective of this battle.

While Darius and Alexander each used a different battle plan—one choosing encirclement and the other penetration—the goal of both strategies was the same. Both sides hoped to destroy the cohesiveness and will to fight of the opposing forces. Killing and wounding their enemies was one means of achieving this aim, but not the only one. Alexander's drive to the center did not in itself cause many deaths. Its success was no less devastating and effective, but it was achieved through surprise and psychological insight. The goal of each army was to destroy the capacity of the other army to resist—and Alexander accomplished this with great efficiency.

The day after the battle, Alexander's victorious army marched south to Babylon, to enter in triumph the city that had been the capital of half of Darius's empire. Babylon was an often-conquered city, and its governor and people were not interested in fighting. After all, reports from other conquered territories said that Alexander was a good ruler; he respected the traditions and religions of his new subjects.

Upon reaching Babylon, Alexander and his troops

settled in. The men were free to nurse their wounds, mourn their dead comrades, buy new supplies with their battlefield loot and take up with any willing Babylonian women. They ate and drank and slept, and told and retold tales of their valor. But for Alexander, lodged in the six-hundred-room palace of Nebuchadnezzar, there was little time for relaxation. Alexander was busy arranging for the government of the new territories, deciding how to reward the men who had fought for him in battle and acting as a court of final appeal for both his new subjects and his army. He also had the task of determining the extent of the supplies and treasuries he had just acquired.

Scarcely a month later, Alexander began preparing for the next stage of his conquest. By early winter he was ready, and he and his army moved on, following Darius and his Persians into the cold highlands of Parthia. From there, after Darius was dead, Alexander pushed even farther to the east, and followed the Indus River all the way to the Indian Ocean. There he paused to pay homage to the gods, and then turned toward home.

Alexander was relentless in his pursuit of power and wealth. He fought and defeated all who would resist him, persisting in his habit of personally taking part in every battle. He shared the hardships his men endured, and suffered wounds to his leg, his shoulder—even one to his chest, through his ribcage and his lung. But Alexander could not stop. He had new cities to found, new governments to establish.

Alexander had an awesome, never-finished plan: to

rule over a united Mediterranean and Asian empire, virtually all of the known civilized world. And, after many years in relentless pursuit of his ambitions, he came again to Babylon. By then he was tired, his body worn down from too many battles and—during this part of his life—too much drinking. Still, Alexander gave himself no rest. There was too much to do; he was making plans to conquer the Arabian peninsula.

But he never accomplished this goal. In Babylon he suffered a final blow to his health, a "swamp fever" he is said to have caught while swimming in some marshes near the city.

Alexander the Great—fabulously wealthy ruler of Greeks, Egyptians and Persians, and perhaps the boldest and most extraordinary military leader of all time—died after a ten-day illness. He was only thirty-two years old.

Alexander sacrificed comfort, sleep, ordinary enjoyments, family life—everything. He went into battle repeatedly, each time risking his life. And at his death he was still unsatisfied. Why would a man do what Alexander did? And why have so many others made similar sacrifices?

Alexander did not hate Darius. When he accidentally captured Darius's mother and wife, he treated them with great honor; he later married one of Darius's daughters. And when one of Darius's brothers surrendered to Alexander in battle, Alexander confirmed him in his lands and made him the head of a special Persian cavalry unit. Moreover, once he had made a conquest, Alexander rather quickly started to learn the language and customs of the people he had conquered.

Obviously Alexander did not think that the Persians represented an evil force that had to be eliminated. Unlike neolithic tribesmen, he did not believe his opponents had to be destroyed to maintain the appropriate balance of cosmic forces. Instead, Alexander understood Darius as simply another human being, an insight that helped Alexander devise a successful battle strategy.

Alexander's goal was simple. He wanted to secure more wealth, power and prestige, for himself and for the aristocrats who fought with him. Destroying an opposing army and replacing it with his own forces was the means to increase the territory he ruled, the taxes he could collect and the place he would occupy in history.

In a typical neolithic war, wealth and land and power do not change hands. But when Alexander was successful in warfare, they did. Not only did Alexander fight in a fashion different from neolithic warriors, he fought for a different goal. What had happened to bring about such a change?

The critical event seems to have occurred three or four thousand years before the time of Alexander. About that time, men and women created a new social system: the state. The word "state" sometimes means California or Alabama or Nebraska, one of the states which together make up the United States of America. But the term also stands for a very specialized kind of governing institution.

The development of the state was not the same as the discovery of a new way of harvesting food or making tools. Instead, it was a new way of organizing people's relations with one another.

Tribal people like the Ojibway or the Yanomamo do not create "states." Rather, all the adult males participate directly in decision making. Economic and social relations are determined by time-honored traditions to which everyone assents. These traditions are, in effect, the rules for living. Both power and wealth are distributed fairly equally. Individual wrongdoing is dealt with by the tribe in an informal fashion.

When humans create a state, they delegate power to specific people and the formal systems that we think of as "government." The people in charge of government make decisions about such things as wars and taxes, and they establish laws. These rulers have armies and police forces to enforce obedience to the laws. In order to undertake large, common projects—building canals or roads—and to collect taxes, rulers must have record-keepers and other specialized workers. Therefore, the establishment of the state brought about the creation of government bureaucracies.

Living under the government of a state had some drawbacks, but it also had many advantages. The most important was a great increase in human power and wealth. Societies were no longer confined to the small size of tribes, three hundred or four hundred people who could all know one another and feel they were part of a single family. Instead, people now belonged to much larger groups. States could govern great numbers of people who might never see or know one another. By coordinating their activities, the state made it possible for humans to carry out projects that were impossible for tribes.

Some of the earliest states were in Mesopotamia, Egypt and China, areas where water was both a problem and an advantage. The need to control floodwaters may, in fact, have helped to create the first states.

Controlling the rivers was a real challenge, something that could not be accomplished by any single tribe or village. The state with its bureaucracy was a means of organizing people living along hundreds of miles of riverbank and requiring them to cooperate in building dams and canals and irrigation ditches. (In Egypt, the farmers derived another benefit once they were under a centralized government. There were official priest-astronomers to tell them when the Nile was scheduled to flood and when it was time for the waters to recede, leaving behind an annual gift of rich soil.)

There were many ways in which the organization of the state led to increased prosperity. Farmers planted more crops, because now they could take the extra food to a central market. People no longer had to rely on just the products of their own village and began to develop specialized skills. Cities grew around the marketplaces and around the great temples, or the courts of the king.

The creation of the state, unfortunately, had negative consequences as well. In particular, the prosperous cities, with their surplus grains and rice, fancy goods and golden jewelry, attracted thieves and other criminals. Typically, new kingdoms had to defend themselves against tribes of nomadic cattle raisers. These tribes, with their wandering life, could not maintain large reserves of food or support specialized craftsmen. Some of the nomads traded with the farmers and city dwellers, but many decided that raiding was easier and provided more gain.

At first, the citizens of the new states fought in their own defense. But it eventually became clear that specialized fighters—like specialized craftsmen—were more effective. Moreover, the existence of professional armies meant that farmers and craftsmen didn't have to interrupt their regular routines in times of danger. So rulers were given the right to levy additional taxes to support permanent trained armies.

There were other drawbacks to the development of the state. The relative equality of tribal life was replaced by great differences in wealth and power. A few wealthy people controlled the land and the kingdom. They gave orders and collected taxes and rents. Other people worked for them. The ordinary craftsmen, farmers, servants and slaves were poor by comparison to their aristocratic rulers. And they were expected to be very obedient.[2]

The new professional armies made it more difficult for the people to prevent a king and his nobles from misusing their power. Unarmed and untrained civilians learned that it was usually wise to obey. In addition, the new armies could also be used to extend control over the nearby lands of other states. This, undoubtedly, is the point in human development when wars of greed began—wars intended to increase the power and wealth of already powerful and wealthy ruling groups.

This new type of warfare was far more costly and destructive than the ritual warfare of primitive agricultural tribes. Neolithic wars, in a sense, were "ecologically sound." Though battles were constantly fought, neolithic warfare did little damage to the land and caused the death of relatively few people. The armies and battles of the new states were much more devastating. Thousands of men might die in a single day—and the land over which they marched and fought might well be useless for at least a year.

And yet the motive for such wars—greed itself—created some built-in limits to the strategy of such warring states. Since a ruler would wish to possess and enjoy the land and people his armies fought for, he would not want to destroy them. Only the organized army was the enemy. Civilians and property, on the other hand, were to be protected and preserved if at all possible. Thus Alexander, for example, forbade any looting in Babylon. Instead, he reconfirmed all the city's ancient rights and privileges, and even made a substantial offering for the rebuilding of its main temple.

But there was no limit to the number of wars a ruler might fight. Indeed, greed created a new cycle of warfare that was almost as predictable as the ritual warfare of neolithic peoples. Greed resulted in the continual growth and collapse of empires. States struggled to expand their boundaries and increase their power, and the successful ones expanded into ever-growing empires. Sooner or later these empires could no longer be controlled by a centralized government and so collapsed into small warring kingdoms. The cycle was ready to begin again.

It is wars of greed that fill our history books.[3] Alexander the Great was but one of the early empire builders. From the epic wars of biblical times to conquests of kings like Louis XIV of France and Frederick the Great of Prussia, the same pattern of events continued.

War fought on home territory invariably meant hardship and grief for the civilians who tried to continue their everyday, ordinary work as armies trampled over their fields, disrupted peaceful trade routes or took food and supplies. Not surprisingly, peasants often banded together to attack undisciplined armies if they were destroying scarce local resources. An aristocracy—if it failed to defend its own territory—often found itself facing rebellion at home as well as danger abroad. But the outcome of a war did not affect farmers and craftsmen very much: They were going to have to pay traditional taxes and rents in any case, no matter to whom, and wars did not increase their income.

It was only the ruling kings and aristocrats, and the mercenary soldiers, who actually had a chance to gain anything. Soldiers would pick up both their pay and the loot left by a defeated enemy; they might even hope to get a special bonus or plot of land if they accomplished some outstanding feat of bravery. And the king and his nobles would find themselves in possession of more land and more subjects—and more taxes and more rents.

Why were the kings and aristocrats so greedy? These rulers of states had every luxury the world could then provide. They were what we would consider extraordinarily rich people. Some were content, of course, but there were always greedy ones, and they were the rulers who set out, like Alexander, to gain as much as they could. Such people gave up ease and comfort for more wealth and power. Like many people today, they pursued wealth relentlessly, seeking more than they could ever personally enjoy. Alexander is considered by historians to be a great man—but his motive, his sense that it was his "destiny" to conquer the known world, is seldom questioned, because his actions are considered to be "natural" and perfectly logical. But are they?

We have very confused attitudes about greed. Sometimes we approve of it; sometimes we don't. We cheer for the person lucky enough to win a lottery, or hardworking—or devious—enough to build or gain control of a huge corporation and thereby acquire great wealth. Some of our most popular novels and television programs are stories about how people have gained enormous amounts of money and power.

At the same time, children who won't share their toys or who grab all the candy are generally disliked and disapproved of. Adults scold them, and other children avoid them. People were horrified at the extravagant spending revealed when the Marcos dictatorship in the Philippines was overthrown. (Imelda Marcos had over three thousand pairs of shoes stored away in her palace in Manila!) We begin to wonder if people who have an uncontrollable need for wealth, power and material goods aren't really "sick."[4]

There are differences between what people truly need and what they come to believe they must have. We know that all living creatures have some basic and genuine needs. Staying alive and continuing the species requires air, water, food, shelter and sexual partners. But these real wants have limits; they can be satisfied. A bear, for example, can occupy only one cave during a winter. It can consume only so much food and water, and can produce only a limited number of cubs. Once a bear's needs are met, it is quite content. It will enjoy life, spending its time sleeping, sunning or playing. It will never kill another bear just to acquire a second cave.

Humans—and many animals—also need nonsexual physical contact. Zoo animals spend much time cuddling and grooming each other. Humans have this social need too, as well as a need to be with others in much more complicated ways. Humans fill this need by sharing ideas and customs—stories, dances, rituals and songs. We seem also to need to attach order and meaning to the things we do, and so we decorate tools and weapons, arrange our homes in certain ways and adorn our bodies.

Unfortunately, as human societies have evolved since the early hunters and gatherers, we have lost much of the direct connection between what we genuinely need and what we do. The first disconnection came with the necessity to plant crops or tend animals, when people learned to work at tedious tasks to provide for future needs rather than for their immediate requirements. This resulted in the neolithic personality, with its emphasis on anger and revenge. But there was relatively little greed among neolithic tribes. In fact, if individuals had more food or possessions than they needed, custom called for the surplus to be distributed to others in the tribe; in other words, *they shared.*

All this changed when people began to live in states rather than in tribal communities. In even the earliest states, there was an enormous expansion of the capacity to produce food and other goods. There was also an expansion of what people felt they needed. In other words, people became greedy. And they thought of their greed as natural. It was a characteristic and "normal" trait of their society.

As with the increase in resentment and vengeful feelings that accompanied the shift from hunting and gathering, the increased greediness of civilized peoples appears to have its roots in changes in the family structure that went along with the creation of the state.

This newer society was a hierarchy. Like a modern-day army, which is also a hierarchical organization, it was divided into ranks or orders. Just as an army is an organizational pyramid, with a few four-star generals at the top and lots of ordinary privates at the base, these societies had a monarch at their peak and peasants or slaves as their base. Nobles and priests, merchants and craftsmen (like officers and noncommissioned officers in an army) filled in the center of the pyramid. These new states, however, differed from a modern army in one crucial way—typically, one was *born* into a rank.

Each rank had its special rights and privileges, and its special duties. For example, noblemen didn't have to pay taxes, but they were expected to serve in the king's army or his bureaucracy. Moreover, each rank owed obedience and reverence to members of the higher ranks, and could expect obedience and reverence from members of the lower ranks. Thus, the nobility of Persia had to prostrate themselves when they entered Darius's presence, but they could also expect a commoner to bow humbly when entering *their* presence.

In such a society, obedience is an essential survival skill, since a refusal to obey a superior could mean harsh punishment or even death. Fathers and mothers of every class therefore attempted to impart this skill to their children. As a result, family structures changed; like the state, they became rigid, depended on assigned roles and emphasized obedience.

Within the family, roles and authority were based on such things as gender and order of birth. Imagine being a child in such a family: Fathers had complete control of wives and children, including grown sons, just as their rulers had complete charge of the state. (Families in which the oldest male is in charge and property passes from father to son are called patriarchal. Patriarchal families developed with the invention of the state.)

Fathers now kept a distance from their children, emphasized their superiority and power and dealt with children in formal ways. Children were given very little cuddling or physical petting after they were about four or five years old, and disobedience was immediately punished—usually by a beating. Patriarchal fathers expressed concern for their children mainly by teaching them how to act appropriately in this rigid, class-structured and authoritarian society.[5]

Children were, moreover, expected to imitate the formality and reserve of their parents, especially their fathers, who demonstrated approval and love only by giving gifts. Material objects became the symbols or substitutes for affection and loving caresses; a child's unsatisfied—and limitless—desire for close, loving contact became focused on material objects. But because gifts and objects can never provide the same feelings of love and approval that hugging and other signs of affection can, the need is never satisfied—and that unsatisfied need becomes an endless desire for *things*. As a result, greed became "natural."

People in our society often behave in ways that are similar to those of the traditional patriarchal familes. Some parents, even though they may be very well-meaning, don't hug their children often or spend much time with them. Instead, they give presents: toys or candy, new clothes, money to spend. Indeed, parents may work especially long hours, hold several jobs or go into debt in order to be sure their children have "everything." Such gifts, *when substituted for direct experiences of love and affection*, are never completely satisfying. Children raised in this manner tend to become adults who can never have enough.[6] Alexander may have been such a person.

People who are disconnected from—even unaware

of—these genuine needs will push on and on in search of satisfaction from material goods. Thus, the merchants and craftsmen of traditional cities struggled to acquire possessions. They worked long hours in their shops and they undertook long, dangerous journeys to acquire gold by trading. Like Alexander, they sacrificed comfort and risked their lives to gain more than they could ever use or enjoy. And peasants were no different. They struggled at their own level—to work more land, to enlarge their meager houses and to acquire bigger families and herds of animals.

Of course, if we interpret this as simply a desire to improve their standard of living or make a better life for their children, we find such striving for wealth very understandable. Such desires are, like war itself, a part of our own cultural norms. But it's important to note they would appear very strange to a hunting-and-gathering people, or to the peaceable Hopi.

The greediness of ordinary people has also been disturbing to traditional elites, though for a very different reason. Once many possessions came to signify "goodness," the ruling classes attempted to ensure that they possessed more than ordinary people. The upper classes in the early states—just as now—had many residences, and each house or castle had many rooms. They accumulated possessions: clothing and jewelry, trinkets, art objects, amusements, servants, gardens and other luxuries. Possessions, including sexual partners, were not limited by the owners' physical capacity to enjoy them.

Instead of being shared, what could not be used was hoarded and denied to others.

So universal, in fact, was this tendency that "sumptuary laws" would periodically be enacted, limiting the amount of wealth and fine clothing ordinary people could display or wear. Rulers wanted exclusive rights to demonstrate their "goodness."

Children of aristocrats and kings, like Alexander, grew up under conditions that were psychologically very similar to those experienced by the children of peasants or craftsmen. They might not have to work in the fields or help their father at the forge, but they did have to undergo years of training from schoolmasters, and they had to participate, silently and carefully, in the formal rituals and festivities of their busy parents' courts. For them, as for ordinary children, material gifts became the substitute for their parents' attention and affectionate contact.[7]

We cannot know for certain, but this seems to be why Alexander the Great was never content. Like many aristocrats of his day, he was raised in a family that was coldly patriarchal. His father had many wives, and Alexander grew up in a quarrelsome, unhappy household. He had very little contact with his father, who spent much of his time building up a huge army. His beautiful mother, Olympias—a very energetic, violent-tempered woman—hated her husband and tried to instill the same emotion in Alexander. Sometimes she lavished affection upon her son, and sometimes she was distant and angry.

Worst of all, she wanted to use Alexander—the king's oldest legitimate son—to further her own greedy ambitions.

Alexander's upbringing, cold and unloving as it must have been, was not essentially different from the upbringing of hundreds of other rulers of his time and after him. For him, as for all those others who were much like him, greed was the logical outcome of his childhood: Being a brilliant military strategist and a natural leader, he set out to conquer the world.

Unfortunately, such greediness can never be satisfied. Since material things are merely a substitute for the love one really wants, one keeps desiring more. For rulers like Alexander—or Julius Caesar, Louis XIV, Frederick the Great or Napoleon—only death or crushing defeat is likely to end their driven attempts to conquer and possess the whole of creation. And so the cycle of greedy warfare between traditional states remained an unending one until very recently.[8]

Twentieth-century rulers and ordinary citizens continue to exhibit greed—for power, wealth or fame—as a "normal" characteristic. But wars of greed have become much less common in this century and, indeed, have almost disappeared. Why?

Just as civilized states found new ways to deal with the desire for revenge, industrialized societies have developed new ways of dealing with human greediness. We have not eliminated greed, but for the most part we have learned to control and exploit natural resources rather than other human beings. We use the power provided by water, coal and oil rather than human power to turn our machines—and we use our machines to create consumer goods in vast quantities. Thus, more efficient ways of production have come to be perceived as the rational way of satisfying people's desire for material goods.

The most recent major war of greed was fought by Japan during the 1930s and 1940s. Japan attacked China and the colonial empires of England, France and Holland, attempting to establish a "Greater Asian Co-prosperity Sphere," which they would dominate—and which, they believed, would increase the wealth of their own country and its ruling class. (American diplomatic objections to this expansionist policy led the Japanese to attack and destroy the United States naval fleet at Pearl Harbor in 1941, in an attempt to eliminate American "interference" in Asian affairs. Instead, the attack led to American involvement in World War II.)

The Japanese lost that war, and since 1945 they have followed a different policy. Limited—by the terms of their peace treaty with the United States—to a very small, police-force-size army, they have devoted their resources and skills to internal technological and scientific development. Moreover, they have achieved, through peaceful economic means, a prosperity beyond the wildest of their earlier dreams.

In effect, though we have not ceased to be greedy, we have discovered more efficient and less destructive methods of appeasing our greediness. Indeed, we have even learned to use our greed to repress some of our warring traditions. For example, the warfare and enmity which for centuries characterized Western European history have over the last thirty years been replaced by the Common Market—an organization of economic cooperation and shared prosperity.

These developments in Europe and Japan give hope for the future. People have learned to deal with greed, as well as the desire for revenge, through peaceful means. Perhaps we can find equally satisfying and nonviolent means for dealing with some of the other motives which have, until now, driven our species into battle.

Chapter Five

Of Joy and Honor

In 1346 the royal armies of England and France met in battle near the town of Crécy in northern France. This was an early battle in what came to be called the Hundred Years War (1338–1453). During this war the French and English kings fought over the right to rule large sections of territory in France. Each wanted this fertile area, across the English Channel from England, which was situated on important trade routes.

Beyond all doubt the long-range motivation for the Hundred Years War was the greed of the French and English royalty. But at Crécy something more was involved than control of territory. While the English fought with an efficiency and purposefulness that Alexander would have admired, the French fought very differently. If we look at the battle closely, we will discover that the French nobility, who comprised the bulk of their king's forces, fought for a different goal and therefore used different tactics.

The English army was commanded by its king, Edward III. His forces were fewer in number than those of the French, so Edward arranged them defensively. He placed his cavalry, his heavily armored men-at-arms with their great horses, in the center of the battlefield. The ground in front of them was lined with stakes pointed toward the enemy, in much the same way that the Emperor Darius had set up his defenses against Alexander. On either side of his cavalry, and slightly in front of them, Edward placed longbowmen. These were archers who had been trained since boyhood to shoot armor-piercing arrows with accuracy and quickness. All of Edward's men, including the noblemen who fought for him, were paid soldiers. He expected them to obey him, and they did.

The French king, Philip, did not control as strong and efficient a state as did Edward. While Edward had an entire army of paid men to command, the French ruler had only enough money to hire a group of Genoese crossbowmen. He had to rely on his noblemen to voluntarily supply the rest of his fighting forces.

These noblemen, while they were subjects of the state ruled by Philip, retained a great deal of independence. They ruled their own manors, had their own sources of income and raised their own small armies. They voluntarily aided their king because it was their traditional duty and right to do so. But they and their men could not be expected to obey commands in the same way that paid soldiers did, and King Philip knew that.

The French king, when he was arranging his army to take the offensive, placed the Genoese crossbowmen at the front of his troops. He expected these hired soldiers to begin the battle with an exchange of arrows that would weaken the British forces. Behind the Genoese waited the independent French nobles. Like the English cavalry, they and their horses were dressed in heavy armor, and they carried long lances and sharp swords. They were to wait until the English forces had been weakened by the Genoese arrows, and then ride out to the attack.

But the battle plan went wrong from the start. The Genoese archers never had a chance to do their job: When the battle started, the first group of French nobles immediately charged forward—riding right through and over the crossbowmen! It didn't matter to the French nobles that the Genoese archers were their allies. They were eager to do battle, to be the first to confront the enemy. In fact, they were irritated that the Genoese—who were foot soldiers and therefore much slower—were in their way.

Once the battle began, unit after unit of the French noblemen charged forward, and each wave was decimated by a hail of arrows from the English longbowmen. Horses as well as riders were killed, and as the French stumbled and hesitated around the bodies of their fallen comrades, English men-at-arms dismounted and pushed forward to kill and take prisoners. Eventually, the surviving French nobles would retreat, regroup and prepare to charge again.

By the end of the day the battlefield was littered with the bodies of the dead and dying. The French king, with a few loyal barons, fled the scene and took refuge in a nearby castle.

What those French noblemen did seems incredibly foolish. By the end of the day almost one third of the French had been killed, primarily by arrows shot by the English longbowmen. And, of course, the English forces won the battle at Crécy.

The French noblemen could—and should—have waited until the Genoese archers had made their task easier. Why did they behave this way? Why were they so eager to charge forward into a hail of English arrows and engage in dangerous hand-to-hand combat?

There was obviously something more important to the French nobles than winning or even surviving the battle. Edward III's son, Edward the Black Prince, understood what this was. After winning a similar battle against the French at Poitiers ten years later, in 1356, he immediately ordered his servants to prepare a formal banquet. He invited his prisoners—the new King of France, his son and many of the French noblemen—to attend. The French, in fact, were to be Edward's honored guests.

The leading noblemen on both sides hurried to wash

By the end of the Hundred Years War, knights and their horses were almost completely armored to protect them from the dangers posed by bows and arrows in the hands of peasants. The Bettmann Archive, Inc.

off the grime of battle and put on their finest clothes. And as soon as all was prepared in Edward's royal tent, the enemies of the day sat down to eat and talk together. No matter that these men had tried very hard during the day to kill each other—the banquet was friendly. The noblemen chatted and told stories of particularly exciting or notable things they had seen or done that day. They would retell these stories many times in the future—especially the parts about acts of bravery and skill.

The nobles constantly complimented one another. Who had won or who had lost was not important. What they all talked about was what they, as individuals, had accomplished. And both English and French agreed that the battle, for all its pain and losses, had been an exciting adventure.[1]

What these English and French warriors did at the banquet after the battle at Poitiers was—in some ways— not unusual. Fighting men have always liked to swap war stories. Even today, soldiers who fought together in World War II hold reunions and retell their experiences. Nonetheless, battles are terrible events during which men often see their friends killed or maimed. Why should soldiers enjoy remembering battles?

War, at least under certain conditions, is a source of pleasure for some of the men who fight.

One of the earliest discussions of the experience of battle is set forth in an epic poem composed almost a thousand years before the birth of Christ by the poet Homer. In the *Iliad*, he told of a war fought several centuries before he lived. This was a war between the Greeks and Trojans, usually called the Trojan War. The hero Achilles is the central figure in Homer's *Iliad*.

When Homer described battles in the *Iliad*, he had to be accurate. Many of the people for whom Homer sang had themselves often experienced similar battles. Any inaccuracies would be challenged by his audience.

Homer tells what happens when a sword cleaves through the helmet and the skull, or how a man sinks down on the ground when a lance gets past his shield and pierces his belly. He spends a lot of time describing Achilles's grief and anger when his best friend is killed, and he also tells of the fear and anguish felt by the parents of the Trojan leader when their son is slain. There is no doubt that Homer and his audiences knew all about the cruelty of the battlefield.

The epic, nonetheless, makes it clear that the battlefield is not just grim. Again and again, in speaking of one of the warriors, Homer will say that the "joy of battle" came upon him. And when that happens, the warrior is transformed, touched—it seems to Homer—by the gods themselves. Homer's descriptions of the experience of battle created vivid pictures in his listeners' imaginations. He told of men who moved with grace and strength, like lions or wild boars. They glowed with energy, he proclaimed, and were like a "fierce fire on some parched mountainside . . . and the wind driving it whirleth every way the flame."[2]

These feelings about the exaltation of battle were also described in 1917 by Pierre Teilhard de Chardin, a priest and scholar who was involved in World War I. At the time, Teilhard de Chardin had been serving for three years on the front lines. He was not a fighting man but a stretcher-bearer who had a great deal of mobility and freedom of action. He was perfectly aware of the destructive side of battle, but he was quite honest about the fascination it held for him.

"The front cannot but attract us," Teilhard de Chardin wrote to a member of his family. "Not only do you see there things that you experience nowhere else, but you also see emerge from within yourself an underlying stream of clarity, energy and freedom that is to be found hardly anywhere else in ordinary life." Teilhard de Chardin added that this exaltation is accompanied by a certain pain. "Nevertheless it is indeed an exaltation. That is why one likes the front in spite of everything, and misses it."[3]

Mary Sinclair, like Teilhard de Chardin, chose to help wounded soldiers. She was an Englishwoman who served in an ambulance unit in World War I. Sinclair had the same response to the excitement of combat: "What a fool I would have been if I hadn't come," she wrote. "I wouldn't have missed this run for the world."[4] Why would such men and women enjoy being in the midst of the danger and suffering of the battlefront—especially in a war as mechanized and destructive as World War I?

In the battlefield's very special circumstances, a person can forget ordinary worries, fears, conflicts and boredom. Men of skill, strength and courage who take part in combat experience intense feelings. They become totally involved and aware *in the present moment*. And that pleasure, the "joy of battle," was most certainly desired and experienced by the noblemen who fought at Crécy and Poitiers—whether they won or not.

It is quite possible to find rewards in warfare, even for those who do not play the warrior hero's role. Others as well, who may never have come near a battlefield—women included—often relish the details at second hand.

All humans enjoy totally compelling situations. Almost everyone has experienced a serious emergency and been called upon to demonstrate strength and resourcefulness. Babies toddle into danger and must be rescued, accidents happen and first aid must be given. For a brief time, nothing else matters. People put all other thoughts from their minds. They don't worry about getting homework done, or how much money they have spent lately, or whom they will eat lunch with next week. Even people who have been feeling bored or depressed an instant before become totally galvanized.

Afterward such people become—instantly—important. They will tell and retell the story to friends and family, who probably also enjoy telling someone else about it. There is an afterglow for everyone to savor. And though people may not be fully aware of it, their ordinary lives seem a bit flat and uninteresting for a while. The experience of acting decisively during an emergency is very similar to the "joy of battle."

Fortunately, such total involvement is not limited to the battlefield or emergency situations. School exams, athletic competitions, musical or theatrical performances and games of skill can also be compelling activities—and are available to everyone. Learning something difficult, such as how to do stunts on a skateboard or how to play a musical instrument, also takes total concentration. Small children easily become totally involved in what they are doing. There are times when it doesn't matter to them if they are cold, or mosquitoes are biting, or their parents want them to come home. They keep right on.

For many older children and for adults, such total involvement is a rare feeling. After all, much of human existence is ordinary and routine. Total involvement temporarily frees us from boredom and disappointments, and from the everyday tug-of-war between what we feel we ought to do and what we want to do.

Total involvement in itself is neither good nor bad. It can give us pleasure, and add excitement and purpose to our lives—but it can create problems for us too. The problems can come about when people develop something like an addiction to intense experiences, in the same way some people become addicted to drugs or alcohol or gambling.

Warriors who enjoy battle are a very special breed. Once addicted to the excitement of battle, they increasingly focus their lives on this particular kind of excitement. They ignore other sources of stimulation and satisfaction.

Some people who have become addicted to the excitement of battle become mercenaries, paid soldiers who search out opportunities for combat and who will fight in any war. Others satisfy their addiction less actively, by reliving past glories. Such people become adept at finding willing audiences; they lead others to share their excitement. Consciously or not, they tempt others to long for a similar high.

Let's go back to what happened after the battle of Poitiers. The banquet that followed that battle obviously allowed the English and French warriors to relive the excitement of the battlefield encounters. But the English prince who hosted the banquet went further than that. After having personally served his royal guests and prisoners, he made a speech in praise of the French prince.

"In my opinion," Edward said, "you have this day acquired such high renown for prowess that you have surpassed all the best knights on your side. I do not, dear sir, say this to flatter you, for all those of our side who have seen and observed the actions of each party have unanimously allowed this to be your due, and decree you the prize and garland for it." (The word "garland" originally referred to a wreath of honor conferred at ancient Greek or Roman games.)

Immediately after Edward made this speech, there were murmurs of praise from everyone. The French said the English prince had spoken nobly and truly, and they said he was "one of the most gallant princes of Christendom."[5] Gallant? He had used mercenary troops and practical tactics designed solely to win a war. He had been trying to acquire more land and wealth; it had been a war of greed!

The French aristocrats, however, had fought for different goals: They wanted glory and honor. Edward understood this. He respected the French nobles and understood why they had acted as they did.

During medieval times—often called the Age of Chivalry—many battles were conducted in the way the French fought at Crécy. This style of combat features a ferocious cavalry charge, followed by a melee of individual duels. Such battles allowed demonstrations of how well and bravely the warriors could fight; each had a chance to display his courage and ability. The objective was to win a prize of honor.

This prize of honor sometimes meant more than wealth—or life itself. It meant the praise of peers, the adulation of spectators, the idealization bestowed by poets. Humans value all of these things, of course; they make us feel good about ourselves. Even more significant, glory, honor and prestige offer the hope of a particular kind of immortality: a place in memory and history.

This promised immortality, along with the desire for excitement and involvement, can lure men to the battlefield; it can blot out their desire to go back to an ordinary life, and even lead them to welcome a "glorious" death. This happened to Achilles, the hero of the *Iliad*. Homer tells us that Achilles wondered at one point whether he should continue fighting or return home. He decided to stay. And Homer tells us one of the motives for this decision. Achilles thought: "If I abide here and besiege Troy, then my returning home is taken from me, I will die here. But my fame shall be imperishable."[6]

Homer wrote glowingly of Achilles's great deeds. Indeed, the *Iliad* is filled with glorifications of war and the warrior. Homer dwells long and lovingly on the beauty of the fighters, their armor, weapons, horses and chariots. He repeatedly—even repetitiously—insists on the courage and skill of the heroes on both sides. But he especially praises Achilles. And, as Homer predicted, Achilles's fame endures to this day.

Sir John Froissart, who recorded the events of the battles of Crécy and Poitiers, was another historian who glorified heroes. He tells us it was his intention to try to record all "the great marvels and the fair feats of arms." He did this, he said, in order that the warriors might be sure of securing "perfect honors and the world's glory."[7] Froissart was successful. The warriors who re-lived the battle of Poitiers at Edward's banquet were given, through his writings, a wide audience for their stories and their self-glorification.

As the battles at Crécy and Poitiers made clear, too great an addiction to glory and the joys of battle can lead to defeat. It is understandable that warriors should want to achieve fame. But why has society been so willing to grant it, even to men who have been defeated? What have warriors done—at Troy, Crécy or anywhere else—that is so valuable?

Heroic warriors bestow a gift upon mankind. They serve as a model, a demonstration that an individual can overcome hardship and danger through courage. The actions of heroic warriors are proof that the fear of death and loss, faced directly in combat, can be overcome.

In one way, heroes play a role similar to that of the Yanomamo's mythical brothers who battled the evil Periboriwa; they exercise control over some small part of a chaotic and otherwise uncontrollable world. But warrior heroes do not seek to control through magic the unseen forces of death and destruction in their world. Instead, they demonstrate that human beings can control their *fear* of death.

Humans have a general anxiety about death, and about their powerlessness against it. But for warrior heroes, this anxiety can be focused on the events of a battle, where there is a specific danger to be met and overcome. Through battle, vague anxieties can be made to disappear—transformed into excitement and a hero's will to demonstrate bravery and endurance. Warriors prove the capacity of humans to handle death and loss by voluntarily confronting these terrible things.

While a warrior hero may not bring his people material prosperity, he does show them what a human can achieve. An ordinary civilian may never fight a battle, but will—inevitably and unwillingly—confront danger, death and misfortune. Warriors who have deliberately chosen a similar confrontation remind civilians that they may find within themselves the same courage. It is for this reason that society bestows upon the warrior his own personal reward: the immortality of glory.

In the past, a warrior's immortality was not easily earned. Warriors had to follow a "chivalric" code and meet certain criteria. For example, the *bushido* code of the samurai—the aristocratic warriors of Japan—taught that an honorable man must be brave, indifferent to pain and suffering, true to his spoken word and unswervingly loyal to his parents, his overlord and his emperor. That is the code of a traditional hero, a code that would have been quite understandable to Homer, Achilles or any of the noblemen who fought at Crécy.[8]

In addition, an honorable warrior does not fight against or kill women and children. Where is the bravery in fighting someone who cannot harm you? Nor does a warrior fight those who are his inferiors. For example, the French nobility at Crécy were contemptuous of the archers. These hired soldiers were not of noble birth. What's more, they fought from a distance and were thus not so individually exposed to danger.

A truly heroic warrior must seek opponents who share his qualities and are his equals—other warriors, who will stretch his ability and bravery to the limit. The hero needs a worthy opponent; he can be heroic only when he fights another hero.

But heroic warriors also respect their opponents; a warrior hero does not see his enemy as evil. In fact, if a warrior does not succeed in killing his opponent in battle, he will accord him full honors in the ceremonies that come afterward.

There is much that we can admire about the chivalric code; certainly it limits the destructiveness and the hatred that war can create. Unfortunately, however, the code of the heroic warrior is not limited simply to the glorification of courage, a willingness for self-sacrifice and respect for one's opponent. According to Morris Janowitz, the foremost American military sociologist, this inherited tradition also involves "a belief in the inevitability of violence in the relations between states, and a lack of concern with the social and political consequences of war."[9] In other words, the heroic tradition assumes that warfare is unavoidable, and that its moral or social consequences are unimportant. These are very comforting assumptions for men whose personal prestige and importance depend on a military career. But peace-loving civilians can and should be more skeptical.

Adherence to the military code has always meant that a fighting man does not need to worry about the impact of his actions on ordinary civilians. When Homer composed his verses about the suffering the Trojan War caused, he did not pay attention to anyone except the heroes and their families. After Poitiers, while Prince Edward and Sir John Froissart took great pains to honor the defeated Philip, neither prince nor historian was concerned about the misery and hardship the battle brought to ordinary peasants and citizens.

In our own century, many German soldiers in World War II clung to the values and honor of the old military code—even though they understood their Nazi government was morally wrong and had brought much suffering to innocent people. Here is what one German officer, descendant of a long line of honorable Prussian military officers, wrote to his wife during the battle of Stalingrad:

I cannot deny my share of personal guilt in all this. . . . I wouldn't think of evading my responsibility; I tell myself that, by giving my life, I have paid my debt. . . . I am not cowardly, only sad that I cannot give greater proof of my courage than to die for this useless, not to say criminal, cause.[10]

Raised by a family that valued the traditional code of the heroic warrior, this man was willing to fight for a government he knew was wrong. Though he believed his actions had involved him in guilt, he was comforted by his belief that by fighting he retained his honor. In fact, he saw his willingness to die as redeeming. It proved his courage.

The tragic feeling that permeates this German officer's letter is quite in keeping with the traditional world of the heroic warrior. Victory, or even survival, was not a requirement for heroic glory. The French prisoners that Prince Edward honored had just lost a battle. Achilles could not keep his best friend from dying, and he himself died before the Trojans were conquered. Success, for the traditional hero and for the society that admired him, was less important than his demonstration of courage— which might be most apparent in his ability to handle defeat.

Homer captures this mood in the final book of the *Iliad*. Achilles is consoling King Priam of Troy, whose son, Hector, he has just killed. He is also grieving for his own father, who will never see him again. He says to Priam:

We'll probe our wounds no more, but let them rest,
though grief lies heavy on us. Tears heal nothing,
drying so stiff and cold. This is the way the gods
ordained the destiny of men, to bear such burdens
in our lives. . . . Endure it then. And do not mourn
forever for your dead son. . . . Rather await some
new misfortune to be suffered.[11]

That mood of calm endurance runs through the great
heroic epics of all traditional cultures. But such a pessimistic view of life is foreign to twentieth-century
Americans—and Soviets. We tend, instead, to have a
"can do" approach to problems and to assume that, with
the right attitude or the correct technology, there is no
problem that cannot be overcome. Thus, we tend to
assume, ignoring the evidence of history, that the true
warrior hero will, ultimately, win. The hero of our
mythic drama, the "good guy," is always successful.

In the history of Western civilization, there have been
two particular periods of time in which the ideals of the
heroic warrior have actually dominated battlefield tactics. One was the time of Achilles and Homer, the so-
called Iron Age of the first thousand years B.C. The other
was the medieval period, which lasted from A.D. 400 to
1350. Both were periods when centralized states were
weak or nonexistent, when armor and weapons were
particularly heavy and expensive and when aristocratic
power was strong. The medieval period was just ending
when the battle of Crécy was fought, which is why there
were two styles of fighting. The English had progressed

further away from aristocratic independence and heroic thinking than had the French.[12]

In our modern world, we are actually far removed from the tradition of warrior heroes and from the code of medieval chivalry. Our soldiers do not routinely sit down in friendship with men they have been trying to kill.

Nor do our soldiers fight only well-armed and well-trained men in hand-to-hand combat. Instead, we use long-distance artillery, missiles and airplanes to attack targets that are almost invisible. In that sense, we are the heirs of the Genoese crossbowmen, not the French nobles. And these long-range weapons are as likely to be directed toward civilians, including women and children, as toward the enemy's army. As S.L.A. Marshall, the sociologist who studied soldiers' firing patterns during World War II, has observed: "The true objective, not only of the atomic weapon, but of rockets and modern bombing fleets, is the physical destruction of a society. . . . We see here . . . a curious transposition whereby the civilian mass becomes the shield covering the body of the military."[13]

We also find the notion of independent decision making during battle unreasonable, and are startled by the actions of the French noblemen at Crécy. Present-day soldiers are expected to obey their officers; they fight as a unit rather than as individuals. A contemporary soldier who behaved like the French noblemen at Crécy would very likely face a court-martial.

Nonetheless, we still value *appropriate* demonstrations

of battlefield bravery. The man who carries out a difficult order in the face of overwhelming odds, or the officer who risks his life in order to save the lives of badly wounded soldiers in his platoon, commands our respect. Individual soldiers who demonstrate such courage under fire receive special medals, are personally praised by the President, have their pictures in the papers and on television. We admire and honor these brave men—even if we disapprove of the war that exposed them to such dangers.

In addition, many people admire the high-level danger and excitement that stories and movies have taught them to associate with battle. They want to share, even if from afar, the warrior's godlike aura of immortality; they envy the heroic fighter his capacity to be so totally alive and so effective. Our craving for adventure and individual bravery is so great that our society continually invents mythical battlefields and larger-than-life warrior heroes.

Movies, television programs and comic books show us a constant parade of brawny men in individual combat. And our "good guy/bad guy" myths continually insist that individual bravery and physical strength can make a difference, can win, can change the world. It's a comforting message for people who, in their daily lives, feel insignificant and relatively powerless.

Yet these invented battle scenes and these tough, individualistic fighters are hopelessly out of date. They bear no relation to the realities of modern warfare on an electronic battlefield. Indeed, the young man who goes off to war expecting to be a brawny, individualistic hero is doomed to disappointment.

For example, America's most recent, if undeclared, war (1965–73) was fought in Vietnam—a small, divided land in Southeast Asia. The United States supported the friendly government of South Vietnam, which was under attack by guerrilla forces supported by the Communist government of North Vietnam. In the last four or five years of that war, one of the major American military goals was to make it impossible for the Communist guerrillas to receive supplies from their allies in North Vietnam. To achieve this objective, however, the United States did not send in American soldiers to engage the enemy in direct combat.

Instead, American pilots blanketed the supply route, a vast area filled with jungle paths linking North and South Vietnam, with millions of tiny sensors. These electronic devices could detect movement, warmth and metal. And these three indications, when taken together, meant a human presence. The sensors transmitted their findings to gigantic computers located in fortified rooms hundreds of miles away.

As Air Force General William Evans explained at a news conference in 1971, the "activation" messages relayed by the sensors were

constantly monitored by an assessment officer in the Infiltration Surveillance Center. . . . From the

activation pattern *the computer* can predict a con-
voy's time of arrival at a point . . . designated as a
strike zone. . . . [This information is] passed to
F–4 fighter-bombers; the pilots enter this data into
the *aircrafts' computers.* This gives the course to
steer . . . and programs an automatic release of the
aircrafts' ordnance.[14]

This might be a description of a video game, except
in one respect: The soldiers are even less active than the
game player. Humans only analyze the data; the computer does the actual plotting and firing.

Since 1971, moreover, electronic military developments have proceeded rapidly, creating, among other
devices, unmanned airplanes that are faster, less vulnerable and just as accurate as manned planes. There will
be little need for physical strength or bravery in a future,
computerized war.

The armies of major industrialized nations, including
our own, are increasingly commanded by managerial
thinkers and staffed primarily by cool-headed techni-
cians. Indeed, the colorful, macho "General Patton types"
have resigned and/or retired from the army in recent
years. According to Otto Kroeger, a psychologist who
has served as a consultant to the United States army,
"the action types, the hard-nosed risk-taking daredevils,
said 'I didn't come to push papers. I joined the action
Army and there's no action.' "[15]

The idea that battle provides a place for demonstrat-

ing individualism and courage is, in fact, a nostalgic illusion. Modern warfare is—like much of life in our
society—technically sophisticated, bureaucratically
managed and physically impersonal. Real war today, no
matter what we may wish to believe, is "antiheroic."

Chapter Six

"New and Improved"—How War Was Modernized

In the early-morning hours of August 15, 1863, a seventeen-year-old Japanese student named Togō Heihachirō slept peacefully in his parents' house in Kagoshima, a small port city on the island of Kyushu. Heihachirō (Peaceful Son) had gone to sleep with the calm assurance of an aristocratic warrior raised in a traditional society. He was the son of the honorable Togō samurai family that had for centuries served the daimyo, or overlord, of his province in the Divine Empire of Japan.

Heihachirō was certain that he understood the nature of the world he lived in and the place he would occupy in it. As his father's life had been, so had his great-great-grandfather's, and all the ancestors before them. Heihachirō was sure his life would follow a similar unchanging pattern, in a stable and orderly world.

But this was not to be.[1]

Just before dawn, Heihachirō's father shook him awake. "Get dressed quickly." His father's voice was urgent. "The militia has been called out to defend the city against those English barbarians."

For Heihachirō, trained since he was twelve to be a heroic warrior, this was a momentous summons. He had no doubts about the sacredness of his cause. He had been only a small boy when the American admiral Matthew Perry had sailed into Tokyo Bay and demanded that Japanese ports and cities be opened to foreign commerce.

To the younger Togō that demand had been disgraceful. Westerners, however, viewed Admiral Perry's actions as perfectly reasonable and, indeed, civilized. The "instincts of nature" and the "natural law" impelled— a British writer, Charles MacFarlane, argued—an invasion of Japan and an end to its isolation. Such use of violence in a time of peace seemed quite reasonable. In the words of Senator Willie Magnum of North Carolina, the Perry mission was necessary because one must "deal with barbarians as barbarians."[2]

Heihachirō, of course, did not think of himself as a barbarian; he saw Westerners as the barbarians. According to his history lessons, Perry's demand violated imperial Japanese policy. In 1600, the emperor and his chief military lord, the shogun, had decided that foreign commerce threatened the traditional way of life in Japan. The emperor and the shogun had, therefore, expelled all foreigners and withdrawn from overseas commerce.

By doing this, they had established a peace unbroken in all the generations since.

Heihachirō also knew that the present shogun had given in to Admiral Perry. His father and his friends were angry when they spoke of this, and talked of Perry as a foreign devil. It seemed to Heihachirō that now at last the foreigners were to be handled correctly. The overlord of Satsuma province, his daimyo, had decided to ignore the cowardly decision of the shogun. He would reject the ultimatum that had been presented by the commander of the English ships anchored in the harbor of Kagoshima and fight the foreigners.

Togō hoped that he would handle himself well when he fought to defend the harbor. After all, he had been taught all his life that he must revere and live by the *bushido* code of a true warrior.

In the dim morning light young Togō dressed quickly. He wore the proper garb of a samurai, a long trousered uniform that fitted tightly around his calves. He carefully adjusted his sword in its belt and picked up his musket. He was particularly proud of the musket and kept its engraved brass fittings gleaming like gold. It was an exact replica of the one his ancestor had used in the emperor's service in 1584.

Heihachirō was assigned to one of the clusters of guns that protected the harbor. As he hurried to his post, he greeted his comrades. He and the other young men were filled with an ambitious excitement, thinking of how they would expel the devil foreigners.

The morning wore on. The daimyo's servants were

making a final diplomatic visit to the British flagship, and so the young men waited. But soon the sky turned hazy and the air became oppressive, unmistakable signs of an approaching typhoon. Divine forces would protect them and the gods would give them victory, Heihachirō thought. After all, had not a divinely sent typhoon defeated the fleet of the mighty Kublai Khan centuries earlier?

But the English, using ships built to withstand ocean storms, ignored the typhoon. Even as the sky darkened and the winds blew the waters of the harbor into foaming whitecaps, the English ships formed into a line of battle. Then they sailed the length of the Kagoshima waterfront, firing in turn on each of the fortifications that lined it.

Heihachirō and others who manned the waterfront guns fought bravely and determinedly. Some tended furnaces behind the gun emplacements, heating the solid cannonballs. Others stood at the mouths of the guns, loading them first with gunpowder and then with the hot cannonballs. Still others waited for the right moment to aim the cannon and insert the burning wick that would cause it to fire.

As he carried balls from furnace to cannon, Heihachirō became hot, sweaty and dirty from the black smoke. His sword and musket lay in a pile with everyone else's; the young fighters had quickly learned that they only

The Japanese navy, in 1904 at the Battle of Port Arthur, used newly acquired Western technology to defeat a large European nation—Russia. (following pages)
Culver Pictures

got in the way. This was all very impersonal; he couldn't even see the enemy he was trying to kill. In no way did this match his expectations of heroic combat!

The samurai warriors tried valiantly to destroy the English fleet. Japanese cannonballs, however, damaged only what they hit; they might break a mast, punch a hole in a deck or take off a man's head. But the English were using missiles unlike anything the Japanese had ever seen. Their cannonballs were not solid, but hollow shells filled with explosives and small iron balls. When the English projectiles hit, they exploded and scattered shell fragments, bits of metal and fire. Small boats near the bank were blown to pieces; the sides of forts exploded into the air and collapsed into ruins.

Even though their ships bucked and turned in the increasingly turbulent waters, the English outfired the Japanese. And many of the English shells landed in the town of Kagoshima itself—no one is certain whether the storm-tossed ships could not control their aim or if the English deliberately shot beyond the waterfront gun emplacements. The fragile Japanese houses were crushed. Fires started, and then the winds of the typhoon picked up each little flame and fanned the fires onward. Everything seemed to be ablaze.

Finally, at dusk, the English fleet pulled back out of range of the shore guns and settled down at anchor to ride out the storm. But the next morning, after the storm had passed, they sailed back into Kagoshima harbor and demolished the remaining Japanese guns. Only then did the English fleet sail away.

Despite all the devastation wrought by the English guns, Heihachirō's mother welcomed the men of her family home as victorious warriors. Throughout Kagoshima, in fact, the citizens were exalted. They had beaten off the English fleet!

But the English were not beaten; they had never intended to land at Kagoshima. They were not interested, as Kublai Khan had been, in conquering the islands and governing them. All they wanted was the right to trade in Japan and convert the Japanese to Christianity.

It was not important to the English that their objectives might require the Japanese to reorganize their government and abandon traditions. Like any other Western nation at that time, the English were convinced that their way of life was better, more progressive and more civilized.[3]

When the bombardment of Kagoshima failed to provide immediate improvement in Japanese treatment of foreigners, a second attack was launched the following year. A fleet of English, French and American ships destroyed the fortifications at Shimonoseki harbor. This time the Japanese gave in—and even had to agree to pay for the cost of the two naval expeditions!

Heihachirō, along with the other samurai warriors, eventually had to recognize that the battle at Kagoshima was not a victory at all. It was a defeat. The truth was that they could no longer defend their beloved homeland and its sacred way of life. Japanese technology had fallen behind the foreigners' to a disastrous degree. They knew now that change of some sort had to occur.

Until Japan had the strength to resist the foreigners and regain control of its destiny, the country would have to tolerate the intrusions and demands of the barbarians. Indeed, it must do more than merely tolerate them. If it was to preserve the traditional way of Japanese life—decreed by the gods themselves—Japan must learn from the West.

In 1866, three years later, Togō Heihachirō enlisted in the newly formed Japanese navy. In 1869 he began to learn English. And two years later, now a young man in his twenties, he sailed for England, where he was to spend seven years learning Western methods of fighting—and new ways of thinking.

It had been over 250 years since Japan had deliberately cut itself off from contact with the outside world. In that time the West had developed a whole new way of life, and of warfare. In just one small part of a lifetime, Togō Heihachirō—and all the Japanese—faced the task of catching up.

Western civilization by the 1870s was radically different from any other civilization the world had ever known. New methods of production based on scientific knowledge and industrial technology had created a great abundance of civilian goods as well as deadly military weaponry. Centralized Western governments could organize both weapons and manpower with great efficiency.

Starting in the 1500s, Westerners had deliberately used scientific knowledge to increase the effectiveness of weapons. Military work was blended with other research by a long line of engineers, mathematicians, chemists and physicists. The astronomer Galileo Galilei, for example, worked out some of his groundbreaking laws of dynamics while attempting to predict how a cannonball would fly through the air.

A multitude of scientific discoveries continued to produce ever more sophisticated fortifications and siege operations, as well as more effective gunpowder and stronger cannon metal. And even as Tōgō studied in England, a Swedish chemist, Alfred Nobel, was developing a new explosive—TNT. This invention, by the end of the nineteenth century, had revolutionized the battlefield. Nobel became an arms manufacturer, and also a millionaire.

There were other changes with which the Japanese had to catch up. By the late 1600s, the powerful kings of Europe had begun to work for standardization and centralization in all areas. Along with this came not only new techniques for producing the weapons of war but also new methods of training soldiers.

The manufacture of weapons, once individually constructed by craftsmen, changed. Muskets, cannons and shot began to be made in standardized sizes. Soon artillery was produced with interchangeable parts. Not only were problems of repair and supply simplified, but the steps in the production of a gun could be divided and given to different workers. Production was faster if one man made only stocks, another barrels, a third triggers and so on. Indeed, most of the earliest factories were devoted to military needs.

The makeup and training of armies also changed radically. The rank and file of armies, instead of consisting of an elite like the men who fought at Poitiers and Crécy, were increasingly drawn from the unemployed of city slums and overcrowded rural areas. And the training of these new soldiers was forced upon them by brutal discipline—floggings and beatings that could kill or scar a man for life.

The training also emphasized minutely regulated drills, performed to drumbeats. Individual bravery or intelligence counted for nothing. Men had to respond efficiently to commands and move according to rigid and complicated patterns. Soldiers, taught to fear their officers more than the enemy, were deliberately turned into robots, efficient cogs in a military machine.

The way military forces were organized also changed, becoming much more complicated and formal. The military, in fact, became the earliest area of European governmental activity to be fully subjected to what is now called "bureaucratic" organization. (Today in the United States, the military is the largest governmental bureaucracy.)

Military tasks were divided up logically and assigned to special commands and units: Some men were prepared for actual battle, while many more worked at other necessary tasks. Some people planned logistics, that is, the means for stockpiling and maintaining weapons, food and other supplies, and having them in the right places at the right times. Others kept up current maps and information; still others planned strategies for all kinds of possible future wars. Also, officers advanced up a strict hierarchy of positions on the basis of education, experience and demonstrated ability. While bravery and leadership were still important, other kinds of competency and specialized skills came to be equally valued.[4]

Until the end of the 1700s, the effect of these changes was limited.[5] The governments of the various European kings seldom could raise enough money to maintain really large armies. But after the French Revolution in 1789, the new government granted all male citizens equal rights and established elected, representative bodies. A government that depended on the consent of the governed turned out to be potentially very powerful. Citizens who felt that the government reflected their own interests and desires were more willing to be taxed, and also willing to be drafted into military service.[6] In earlier times, for example, even a powerful monarch like Louis XIV could maintain an army of only about 200,000 men. But Napoleon, profiting from the political changes created by the Revolution, could draft 100,000 young men a year. In 1812, when Napoleon invaded Russia, he led a Grand Army of 500,000 men—and an equal number remained behind to maintain his conquest of Spain and Portugal.[7]

At first, monarchs and aristocrats were horrified by the egalitarian character of the French Revolution. But the increased state power it offered was attractive. As a result, during the nineteenth century, more and more European states imitated the new political organization brought about by the French Revolution.

At the same time as the political revolution in France, the English began an equally dramatic industrial revolution. Nonhuman sources of power—water, coal and steam—came into use, as did specialized machinery capable of manufacturing other machines. The same number of people could now produce much more, and at less cost. Transportation, too, rapidly became faster and cheaper, as steam was used to power railroad trains and ships.[8]

In addition to its impact on civilian life, the Industrial Revolution made possible radical changes in military operations. Military equipment and weapons were cheaper and more effective. Armies were no longer tied to the pace of a horse or an ox; navies were freed from their dependence on changeable winds.

By the middle of the 1800s, when Tōgō Heihachirō came to England to learn Western ways, the new developments had come to seem natural and even inevitable. Human ingenuity seemed to have provided the instruments of power that allowed people to use the "laws of nature" to their own advantage. Western leaders, looking back over the events of the last few centuries, now acted on some new ideas about the nature of reality.

The first of these new theories concerned the place of war in history and its relation to cosmic truth. There had been many changes in the ways men fought and prepared to fight, and there were also changes in beliefs about the meaning and value of war.

Consider what Togō Heihachirō had learned as a boy—that a true samurai fought to preserve social harmony as well as his personal honor. According to what young Togō believed, the proper structure of society reflected the will of heaven: it was holy and unchanging. Honorable violence never attempted to change that order, only to restore it.

Similarly, the ancient Romans believed that the only legitimate war was a *just* war. By *just*, they meant a war fought to defend and preserve the way things were. Moreover, they believed that only a just war would be crowned with success by the gods. These ideas were shared by many traditional civilizations; they were an extension of neolithic beliefs about war as an instrument for overcoming chaos.

However, since they were motivated by greed, the Romans and the Japanese did not always fight "just" wars, or wars to keep things as they had always been. As a result of their victories or defeats, boundaries were changed, other peoples were conquered and different political and social relations developed.

Nonetheless, belief in divine justice or harmony continued. This meant that an aggressor had to convince himself that he was acting to preserve the proper order of things. Alexander, for example, managed to convince himself that he was semidivine, that his true father was a god. His conquests, then, became part of an immortal destiny. On the other hand, Roman warriors tended to see their conquests as the unintended result of a just defense. This is particularly noticeable in the history Julius Caesar wrote about his wars. Though his conquests almost doubled the size of the Roman Empire, he insisted that each battle had been forced on him by the unprovoked aggression of the Germanic tribes he conquered.[9]

Finally, according to traditional thinking about war, each war should—and people insisted it did—reflect a divinely established justice. This meant that each war should, ideally, have been the final war. Its results should have lasted for eternity.

During the eighteenth century, however, Western civilization had developed a different theory and a different understanding of the cosmos. People had come to believe that change was a good thing. In fact, they thought that it was necessary and inevitable. After all, they had experienced enormous changes in their own lifetimes—and most of these felt good. So they abandoned the myth that the heavens had decreed a single, eternal structure for the human world. Instead, they believed that humans were destined to create ever-better systems of living.[10]

In the middle of the nineteenth century, the idea of progress took on another aspect. In 1859 Charles Darwin published *On the Origin of Species*. This book seemed to provide scientific confirmation for the belief that war, in particular, was the way progressive history worked its way in the world.

Darwin's work provoked a great deal of controversy

at the time, as it occasionally does today. Not everyone accepted his theory of biological evolution. But even as disputes raged on whether man had "descended from a monkey," other ideas in Darwin's work were easily accepted. Europeans were flattered to believe that the world constantly evolved through struggle toward "higher" forms of life. (Higher, for them, meant Western and Christian ways.) And they believed that the truth of the "survival of the fittest" was proven. After all, Western nations during the nineteenth century had defeated other countries and imposed their will on them without much difficulty.[11]

Europe's increasing domination of the globe made it easy to accept the idea that progress, a good thing, was the result of competition and struggle—in other words, warfare.

This idea was expressed everywhere. When Japan went to war with China in 1895 as part of an attempt to assert its right to trade with Korea, an article in an influential magazine, *North American Review*, commented that the war was "a conflict between modern civilization, as represented by Japan; and barbarism, or a hopelessly antiquated civilization, by China." Of course, in the 1860s it had been the Japanese that Americans characterized as barbarians. But an official report to the American Secretary of State was certain of the worthiness of western civilization's influence. "Japan is now doing for China what the United States did for Japan. She has learnt western civilization and she is forcing it on her unwieldy neighbor."[12]

Western leaders believed a second theory, which followed from the first: If civilization could continually produce more, better and faster weapons, then the greatest firepower and speed would surely produce prompt victory for the side employing it.

The Prussians had drawn this conclusion from their defeat by Napoleon in 1806–7. The great Prussian military strategist Karl von Clausewitz insisted that "all modern war proceeds from Napoleon's views," and that modern war was characterized by its emphasis on *mass multiplied by speed* as the means of "breaking, in a battle sought from the outset of the war, the moral and material forces of the adversary."[13]

Mass times speed created military strength, and so everyone thought the comparative size of armies (men and weaponry), multiplied by the speed with which they could move toward battle, would logically determine which side was victorious. This *mass times speed* theory was widely believed to be a scientific formula.

Indeed, the Prussians used this principle, and beat the French quickly and decisively in 1871.[14] And throughout the nineteenth century, European armies easily defeated the more traditional forces of Asia, Africa and the Near East. Ignoring the differences in technology and organization that had produced their victories, Western military leaders became convinced of the truth of the *mass times speed equals victory* formula. Modern wars would, they believed, be increasingly short and effective; victory would always go to the side that could reach the battlefield first with the greatest amount of firepower.

One immediate result of this new belief was an enormous expansion of the size of armies. With the exception of England, all major countries in Europe established peacetime drafts. All young men were required to spend two or three years in the army learning how to be soldiers. When these years of training were over, they were required to be in the reserves. Reservists had to keep up with their training: Until men reached forty, they spent a month or two with the reserves every year. What's more, they had to be available for fighting whenever the state needed them. By 1914 there were close to 17 million men in the reserve armed forces of the various European states.

Mobilizing these men to fight quickly was, of course, an enormous task. They had to be moved from their peacetime homes and jobs and into military barracks. Then, as rapidly as possible, they had to be taken to wherever military planners thought they would be needed—to the country's borders, or wherever the "front" might be.

Military leaders worried a great deal about how to get their armies to the battlefield as quickly as possible. Such mobilization was a very complex operation. In countries where the major routes of transportation had been rivers and wagon roads only a generation or so earlier, railroads were now a military necessity. Without them mobilization would be impossible. Every general staff developed complete, detailed plans for using the nation's railroad system as efficiently as possible to take troops to battle areas.[15]

A decision to mobilize, then, came to be seen as very much like a declaration of war. Once begun, a mobilization would be very difficult and costly to cancel.

The third theory in this new Western thought predicted that science and technology would continue to produce more and more effective weapons. And, indeed, weapons were continually, and deliberately, improved. Guns became more accurate, more devastating. Naval designers and inventors produced larger, faster and more effective ships. By the 1890s, when Tōgō Heihachirō had become a naval commander, the ships that had so impressed him at the battle of Kagoshima a mere thirty years earlier were out of date—of no more use than his grandfather's musket with its engraved brass fittings had been in 1863. Sails had been replaced by steam engines, wooden hulls were now made of steel and fighting ships had become specialized: Battleships, cruisers and torpedo boats performed very different functions in naval battles. Moreover, people believed that progress and survival meant that research and invention must never be abandoned.[16]

Tōgō Heihachirō, who had become commander in chief of the Imperial Japanese Navy, retired in 1906. In a message to his comrades, he declared that "to promote to an ever greater height of prosperity the fortunes of the country, the Navy . . . must always maintain its strength at sea and must be prepared to meet any emergency. . . . We must plan future developments and seek not to fall behind the progress of the time."[17]

Theodore Roosevelt, then President of the United

States, was so impressed with the "truth" of this statement that he had copies of Togō's farewell address distributed to all officers in the United States army and navy.

The fourth and final nineteenth-century theory had to do with how peace could be preserved. When Admiral Togō made his retirement speech, he ended his remarks by reminding his audience that "heaven gives the crown of victory to those only who *by habitual preparation win without fighting.*"[18] [Italics added.]

Behind Togō's words is the belief that rational nations, after all, will not undertake a war that seems certain to lead to defeat and disaster. Therefore, if a nation is really strong and well armed, that nation will not be attacked.

At the close of the last century, science and experience made these four theories seem logical, at least to many people. And these beliefs were emphasized very persuasively by men who wished their countries to survive and be prosperous. But the events of the summer of 1914—and the decades that followed—cast serious doubts on all those hopes and beliefs.

Chapter Seven

Brutal Fear

A century of relative peace between the major nations of Europe ended quite suddenly, shattered during just a few weeks during July and August of 1914. Five large and militarily prepared nations—England, Russia, Germany, France and the Austro-Hungarian Empire of central Europe—declared war on one another. Then other major countries entered the fight: Japan, Australia, Canada and finally the United States. Before World War I was over, it had become humankind's first global war.

World War I was different from traditional wars, like those of Alexander or Louis XIV, which were generally fought by small elites for territorial gain. In 1914, the people of the countries that declared war were not forced to go forth to battle to satisfy the greed of their rulers.

Rather their elected representatives formally approved the decision to mobilize and fight.

The people *chose* war.

Over 90 percent of the elected representatives of each nation involved approved their country's declaration of war. And people everywhere responded eagerly. Incredible though it seems in retrospect, something like an air of gaiety prevailed. Everyone reacted with enthusiasm and answered the call to arms.[1]

The young people of 1914 were a generation who knew of war only by report; they had no idea of its grim realities. Here's what Vera Brittain, then a young British university student, remembered about the experience: "To me and my contemporaries, with our cheerful confidence in the benignity of fate, War was something remote, unimaginable, its monstrous destructions and distresses safely shut up, like the Black Death and the Great Fire, between the covers of history books."[2] People still believed in progress and the virtues of Western civilization.

In England, young men hurried to enlist lest they miss out on what they saw as a great adventure. These young people couldn't have been aware of the "improvements" that had been made in weaponry while they were young or before they were born. Their knowledge of war, like Togō's, was based on the experience of an earlier time. (Men in other countries were already part of a reserve based on universal conscription, but they also responded to the call-up with excitement and pleasure.) C. E. Montague, later a well-known English essayist, writing about the battalion with which he underwent training in the fall of 1914, reported that men "would agree among themselves to get up an hour before the pre-dawn Reveille to practice among themselves . . . in the hope of approaching the far-off, longed-for ideal of smartness, the passport to France."[3] And since they believed that *mass times speed equals victory*, practically everyone—including national leaders—expected the war to be over by Christmas.

But it wasn't. It went on for four gruesome years.

Unlike the battle at Kagoshima in 1863, in which one side had vastly superior weapons, most of the countries involved in World War I had the same technology available to them. They all had fast-firing rifles, machine guns and heavy artillery. And these weapons forced soldiers to adopt tactics quite different from those used in previous wars.

To protect themselves from these weapons, armies dug into the ground, creating great networks of trenches extending two or three miles behind the front line and stretching in Western Europe from the Swiss Alps to the coast of the North Sea. The soldiers lived in these trenches. Food supplies and medical care were often lacking. The men's boots—sometimes even their feet—rotted in the mud. From time to time one side or the other would try a frontal attack on the enemy's line, but these attacks could not achieve breakthroughs. The defensive power of the machine gun meant that the attacking army would be almost eliminated long before it could gain control of its opponent's trenches.[4]

Faced with a tactical impasse, military leaders on both sides turned to a strategy of attrition—trying to "wear out" the enemy. As a result, huge amounts of ammunition were used, and the loss of life was enormous.[5]

Roland Leighton, a young soldier, described what he had seen in a letter he sent home from the front.

The dug-outs have been nearly all blown in, the wire entanglements are a wreck, and in among the chaos of twisted iron and splintered timber and shapeless earth are the fleshless, blackened bones of simple men who poured out their red, sweet wine of youth unknowing, for nothing. . . . Let him who thinks War is a glorious, golden thing, who loves to roll forth stirring words of exhortation, invoking Honour and Praise and Valour and Love of Country . . . let him but look at a little pile of sodden grey rags that cover half a skull and a shin-bone and what might have been its ribs. . . . [6]

The optimistic young men who had enlisted discovered they were not fated to gallop across the battlefield, conquering the enemy with their superior skill and daring. Instead, they cowered in the trenches, as the air above was filled with shattering, screaming barrages of shells. Or they straggled across "no-man's-land," among shell holes, barbed-wire barricades and a devastating hail of machine-gun bullets.

They died by the thousands.

This kind of battlefield was completely different; it had an unprecedented *feel*. Guy Chapman, an English writer who served in World War I, wrote about what he had seen.

I caught in my glass [binoculars] a grey ant crawling over the edge of the railway cutting, followed by another, and then more. The sun polished their steel helmets into a row of little shining discs. More and more were now coming out of the cutting. . . . They came crawling in three lines, about six hundred strong.

They were just starting down the forward slope when something flashed in front of them. A column of bright terracotta smoke was flung up-wards. . . . Another and another rose until an ar-cade of smoking pillars seemed to move across the hill-side.

Already the grey ants had thinned. The first line was hardly there. It merged with the second and mechanically the whole inclined southwards to avoid the shells. But the guns followed the movement and another line of smoking columns fountained into the air. At last, reduced to one line, the minute figures turned and stumbled back over the crest of the hill.[7]

With this new mode of warfare, something else had changed: the distinctions between soldiers and civilians, men and women, disappeared. An industrialized army's ability to continue fighting depends on the production of armaments by civilians. So in modern warfare, entire populations become a deliberate target of military action. For example, during World War I both sides used submarines and cruisers to cut off enemy supplies—not only the raw materials of war, but food for civilians as well. And the first aerial bombing of civilians occurred during the last year of the war.

The devastation brought by World War I was almost beyond comprehension. By the time it was over, more than eight and a half million men had died on the battlefields, and millions more were permanently disabled. For the victorious side alone, the war involved direct costs of $186,333,637 and indirect costs of another $151,646,942,560—and that was when a dollar was worth at least ten times its current value. Entire economies and ways of living were destroyed. Not surprisingly, by the time the war was over, three of the five governments that began the war had failed to survive it. There had been revolutions in Russia, Germany and the Austro-Hungarian Empire.[8]

Less than twenty years later, however, the countries who had lost or been dissatisfied with the results of World War I again went to war. They were determined to avoid the mistakes of that first global conflict.

But how?

A casualty of the trench warfare of World War I. (following pages)
The Bettmann Archive, Inc.

The leaders of these countries were counting on better technology and better strategy. They thought the answer to the stalemates of World War I would be the tank and the airplane; in other words, modern machines would restore mobility to the battlefield.

Liddell Hart, an Englishman, wrote in the 1930s that with these new machines, a quick victory was finally possible. "The means was to pass powerful columns of fast-moving tanks, strongly protected by aircraft, through the forward areas."[9] It was another way of saying what Karl von Clausewitz had declared a century earlier: *Mass times speed equals victory.*

Hitler and the German generals who read Hart were convinced by his arguments. When they invaded Russia in the late summer of 1941, they didn't even bother to provide their troops with winter uniforms. Like those eager young people who had rushed to volunteer for military service in 1914, they expected everyone to be home for Christmas.

Surprise tactics allowed the Germans to advance deep into Russian territory, but did not give them victory. There were four years of slow, desperate combat. The trenches of World War I were re-created in the rubble-filled streets of Leningrad and Stalingrad. And then, finally, the Russians drove the Germans back out of their country.[10]

Throughout World War II, all the nations involved used airplanes or rocket bombs against the cities of their enemies, trying to undermine civilian morale and support for the war. The American and British air forces, for example, devised methods of bombardment that created "fire storms." These fires were so hot and large that they used up all the oxygen in a city and pulled in more from the surrounding countryside. And, of course, the first atomic bombs were dropped on cities in Japan. More civilians than soldiers died during World War II.[11]

The aftermath of World War II was destruction and disorder. The cities and transportation systems of Russia, Poland and Germany—and to a lesser extent those of France, Italy, Holland, Belgium and England—were a shambles. The United States, whose territory had escaped any harm, poured millions of dollars into the task of helping both friends and foes rebuild their countries.

To this day, most major powers continue to strive for superiority based on technology, i.e., faster intercontinental missiles and bigger nuclear bombs. If there is ever a World War III, it will be even more devastating and destructive than earlier global wars. And while a nuclear war might be quite short, it would involve—like World Wars I and II—a strategy of massive bloodletting. There would be the same failure to distinguish between soldiers and civilians.

Why, then, are people willing to prepare for, initiate and continue wars that inflict such horrendous damage on winners and losers alike—or wars that may mean the end of civilized human life?

Events at the beginning of World War I offer a clear explanation of why people are willing to enter such a war. We know a great deal about the thinking and motivation of the major European leaders in the summer of 1914. All of this is now a matter of open historical record, and this record shows that World War I was very much a war of mutual fear.

Like many wars, World War I was set off by one particular incident—although it probably could just as easily have been some other event. The Archduke Ferdinand, heir to the Austro-Hungarian crown, was assassinated by a group of Serbian radicals; it was the kind of act we would describe today as terrorism.

The ministers of Austria-Hungary decided to use force to punish Serbia, in keeping with their desire to eliminate it as an independent state. In the words of Conrad von Hötzendorf, the Austrian chief of staff, "It was not a question of a knightly duel. . . . It was much more the *highly practical importance of the prestige of a Great Power* . . . which, by its continual yielding and patience, had given an impression of impotence and made its internal and external enemies continually more aggressive."[12]

Russia, on the other hand, decided to mobilize its armies to help defend Serbia—its Balkan cousin—against an Austrian attack. The Russians at the same time decided to move troops to the borders shared with the German Empire. Even though the Germans had not yet decided to mobilize for war, the Russians were convinced, incorrectly, that they were planning to do so. Serge Sazonov, the Russian foreign minister, said that war had been "thrust upon Russia and Europe by the ill will of the enemy, determined to increase their power by enslaving our natural Allies in the Balkans, destroying our influence there, and reducing Russia to a pitiful dependence upon the arbitrary will" of Germany and Austria.[13]

Having learned about the Russian actions, the Germans, just two days after the Russians had ordered mobilization, also began to mobilize—against both Russia and its ally France. They mobilized according to very detailed plans drawn up in the 1890s that called for an immediate invasion—through neutral Belgium—of France. They hoped they would be able to defeat France rapidly, so that they could avoid the dangers of fighting a two-front war.

Here's how the chief of the general staff, Helmuth von Moltke, explained this decision in a conversation with a young aide-de-camp: "Germany can purchase the preservation of peace now only at the price of severe national humiliation. . . . Should Germany now delay this measure [mobilization for war], Germany will enter the war in the most unfavorable conditions. . . . Our military position will become every day more unfavorable and may have the most disastrous consequences for us."[14]

The British, more reluctantly, declared war against Germany. British leaders were convinced that if England "did not help France, the Entente [alliance with France] would disappear; and whether victory came to Germany, or to France and Russia, our situation at the end of the war would be very uncomfortable."[15]

The British feared being isolated. They were also convinced that failure to resist a German violation of Belgian neutrality would leave the British "participators in the sin, the direst crime that ever stained the pages of history."[16]

Only the French had a clear territorial goal for the war. They wanted to regain from the Germans the border province of Alsace-Lorraine, which they had lost in 1871. Moreover, they were glad that their friendship treaty with Russia and England meant that they would not have to fight the Germans alone, as they had in 1871.

The other governments, however, went to war with greater reluctance. They understood that they were risking loss and defeat. But they feared even more what might happen if they remained at peace: "loss of prestige and influence," "severe national humiliation," "disastrous consequences." They sought to avoid isolation and discomfort, defeat and second-rate status. They felt a deep concern for their safety, their prestige and their images as "great powers" or "champions of justice."

World War I was fought out of fear. And fear has remained a primary motivation for warfare and military preparations ever since.

Most people think of Hitler's Germany as a nation intent on world dominance. Hitler, as leader of a country that had been badly defeated in World War I, ranted in public about the strength and invincibility of his new Third Reich.

But in private Hitler was hysterically fearful. "If Germany is to become a world power, and not merely a continental state—and it must become a world power if it is to survive—then it must achieve complete sovereignty and independence. . . . We cannot, like Bismarck, limit ourselves to national aims. We must rule Europe or fall apart as a nation, fall back into the chaos of small states."[17]

World leaders today continue to speak in terms of self-preservation. The United States in the late 1940s was convinced that it was threatened by a Soviet-led "militant minority, exploiting human want and misery . . . to create political chaos."[18]

President after president has essentially acted in agreement with the "domino theory" laid out in a 1947 speech to Congress by President Truman. He put forward the notion that defeated friendly nations could fall, one upon another, in the same way upright rows of dominoes will all fall once the first is toppled. "Should we fail to aid Greece and Turkey in this fateful hour, the effect will be far-reaching."[19] The same "domino" principle has been applied to Korea, Vietnam and Central America.

The Soviet Union was also very explicit in the decade after World War II about its fears. As Premier Khrushchev explained in a 1956 speech, "Soon after the second world war ended, the influence of reactionary and militarist groups began to be increasingly evident in the policy of the United States of America, Britain and France." Such groups, he believed, were driven by a desire "to win world supremacy," and bring about the destruction of all Communist regimes.[20]

The Soviet belief that an attack by hostile capitalist forces was "inevitable" has been modified since 1956. Instead, Soviet military-political doctrine accepts that there would be "no winners" in a nuclear conflict; that "peaceful competition and coexistence" are possible. However, this optimism is based on trust in the strength of Soviet military and economic power. They are determined to sustain that strength by maintaining a mass conscription-based army and giving military goods priority over civilian consumption. It is all, they believe, that protects them from another hostile invasion. (It must be remembered that Russia has been invaded many times; the fear of invasion is based on past experience, not just myth.)

Such fears, universal among powerful modern nations, explain the particularly destructive character of twentieth-century wars.

The desire to eliminate a perceived danger is widespread among living beings. Consider the behavior of a cat threatened by a dog. Avoidance is the natural first response to danger. But if the cat can't eliminate the danger from the dog by hiding or running, then the cat will turn and fight. (This is especially true if it is a mother cat with kittens nearby.) In that situation the cat will turn into a whirlwind of viciousness, lashing out against the threatening dog with tooth and claw. This kind of response is cold and deadly; it seeks to annihilate the danger, to remove it entirely.

In military terms, this is known as the principle of the Death Ground. When soldiers find themselves on Death Ground, they will fight in the same way as a mother cat.

This military principle has been known for thousands

of years. Sun Tzu, a great Chinese military theorist, explained it in 500 B.C. "It is the nature of soldiers to resist when surrounded; to the death when there is no alternative. . . . In a desperate situation, they fear nothing . . . they stand firm . . . they will display immortal courage."[21]

Fear produces results far different from greed. Frightened animals—and fearful humans—do not fight to possess something but to eliminate it. The only goal of aggressive fear is annihilation of whatever has caused it. This motivation is far different from that of Alexander, who wanted to keep Persia as intact as possible because he wanted to possess it.

The psychology of fear is obvious, too, in the development of present-day weapons: atomic, thermonuclear and neutron bombs, as well as all the increasingly rapid and sophisticated means for delivering them to enemy territory. Nuclear weaponry is not the weaponry of greed; its use will leave nothing about which to be greedy. It is, for all who possess it, the weaponry of fear—intended to serve as a deterrent, frightening the enemy into peacefulness. If this does not work, then it will serve as an instrument of annihilation.

The two global wars of the first half of the twentieth century were produced by a widespread and disastrous miasma of fearfulness. It still poisons international relations. Why are we so afraid?

One source of our fear is a widespread and generally shared individual sense of powerlessness and insecurity. The other comes from our belief in the nineteenth-century myth of progress, the theory of "survival of the fittest."

Most people living today share a deep-rooted sense of anxiety; they feel powerless. It is part of the price we pay for living in an industrialized society. Like the shift from hunting and gathering to farming, the shift to industrialization has involved both gains and losses. And again, in spite of the losses, no one really wants to go back to the way things once were.

Would you be willing to return to the monotony, endless labor and short life spans of a preindustrial world? Not likely. Nor do we want to give up telephones, automobiles, hospitals and all the other advantages of modern life—or even the superficial pleasures: Disney World and rock concerts, videos and chocolate-mint ice cream, hair dryers and shopping malls.

But when humans adapted to industrial society and all its luxuries and benefits, they also accepted certain psychic costs. For one thing, the way children were raised had to change drastically. In particular, everyone had to go to school. Education was once the rule for only a few, but now it is the norm for everyone between six and sixteen—and frequently long past that.

Going to school means conforming, sitting still and doing what adults say. And parents and teachers enforce the constrictions of school out of love and concern; they know that conforming to such a regime is necessary for success in adult life.

Except for a small number of people—mostly some artists and athletes—everyone must conform. People of any age who work full-time or part-time know that work in the modern world requires rigid schedules, suppression of emotions, control of physical activity—even artificial sociability. Think about what is involved in being a cashier in a supermarket, a factory worker, a flight attendant or even a doctor.

School may feel constraining at times to a young person, but adults have even less day-to-day freedom. Life in an industrial society involves constant low-level frustration. Just as a student is restricted in school, adults also are restricted by their responsibilities.

The result is an inner reservoir of rage and anger that we almost never acknowledge. Expressing it is too dangerous. Modern people must live and work together in close contact. Expressing that rage and frustration by brawling, screaming and hitting fellow citizens, family members or our co-workers can lead to loss of a job, or a jail sentence.

With international relations, however, we have a stage on which we can indirectly act out our anger—and win social approval at the same time. We can project onto the enemy all the elements in our own character and our own society that are distasteful to us. For instance, during World War II, a German poster characterized the American army as composed of Ku Klux Klan fanatics, jazz-crazed blacks, convicts, hangmen and mad bombers.

The poster attempted to deny that there were any convicts, hangmen or jazz-crazed individuals in the German population or its conscripted army. Such reprehensible characteristics were projected onto America. Moreover, by absurdly lumping together blacks and the racially and religiously bigoted Klan while calling Klansmen "fanatics," the Germans could deny their unconscious fear that their own racist and antisemitic policy was excessive and irrational. Instead they projected those qualities onto a non-German enemy.

At the same time, President Roosevelt assured the Americans that they were fighting for the "victory of the forces of justice and righteousness over the forces of savagery and barbarism."[22] In doing so, he asserted a purity for his own people which ignored the injustice of racial segregation. Instead he projected onto the Germans the "savagery and barbarism" of the American people that had produced waves of lynchings in the 1920s and '30s and were the source of violent antiblack race riots during the war itself.

Even in the absence of outright warfare, we see the enemy as immoral but ourselves as pure. And the enemy is also seen as more greedy than we are. Thus, Americans are sure the Soviets want to conquer and rule us— and the Soviets think the same thing about Americans.

Does this sound similar to the ways neolithic warriors thought about their enemies? It is, but modern thinking differs in one significant way: *We have a much greater sense of personal powerlessness and fear.*

In traditional tribal or agricultural societies, the role any individual was expected to play as an adult was thought to have been divinely ordained. People believed that if they fulfilled their assigned role, they had accomplished something worthwhile. They could be certain of their significance—however tiny—in the universe. And such people lived in small communities; almost everyone received a measure of social recognition, approval and prestige. Life may have felt terribly hemmed in to these people at times—their lives certainly seem so to us—but their conformity did bring rewards and affirmation that they were behaving properly and well.

People who live in industrialized societies, even in socialist states like the Soviet Union, are placed in a much more difficult situation. Adults are seldom allowed the satisfaction of individual achievement. They do not personally build their own homes or educate their own children. Most workers, moreover, don't have the opportunity to complete a project from start to finish; instead, they work on pieces of something. Consumption—the ability to buy impersonally produced things—replaces the satisfaction of nearly all individual achievement.

At the same time, people everywhere are expected to be competitive and to excel. We not only compete with others, we compete with ourselves; past achievements are to be surpassed. Athletes who have broken world records are expected to go on to newer heights in the next Olympics. People never know when they have done enough.

In industrialized societies people feel they are always in danger of being failures. This creates a constant sense of insecure dissatisfaction—of powerlessness. On top of all this, while much value is placed on "rugged individualism," especially in the United States, the reality is that we are all very dependent on others for survival, and we know it.

People alleviate their individual feelings of powerlessness through loyalty to a larger group, the country in which they are citizens. Eventually, people come to feel that though they as individuals may not personally amount to much, their country is the best, the wealthiest, the most important, the most powerful. And—in the U.S.S.R. as well as in the U.S.—we merge our personal identities with that of the larger community.

But we also project upon our society our own sense of powerlessness and our fear of failure. We embody our individual anxiety in the modern myth that warfare determines the "survival of the fittest." We fear that any inability to control the world, any minor defeat, would mean extinction—that we might, like the dinosaurs, disappear entirely.

Thus, the optimistic and reassuring side of the theory of progress is matched by a pessimistic and threatening possibility. People fear—even if in secret—that they or their country may become losers. In a survival-of-the-fittest scenario, the fate of the defeated is a gloomy one. Those who have lacked the courage, ability or willpower to win are unfit, second best, unmanly. Judged and bypassed by history, they will be reduced to insignificance. They will fail to survive.

Survival-of-the-fittest thinking declares that the alternative to greatness and world power status is historical extinction. And the stakes have been escalated by technology. The world of Alexander the Great was but a fraction of the actual world. In our high-technology era of rapid transportation and instant communication, "world power" literally has come to mean influence over the entire planet—and even over space!

All of this makes international relations very frightening. It explains why large, prosperous nations possessing enormous scientific and productive capacity can talk at times as if they were weak and fragile. It underlies statements such as Ronald Reagan's in 1982 concerning El Salvador, a small country: "Failure of commitment there would mean that our credibility would collapse, our alliances would crumble, and the safety of our homeland would be put in jeopardy."[23]

Do we really live in a world of win-or-be-eliminated?

Many nations have been defeated in the twentieth century. Germany and Japan were defeated in 1945. Yet both have gone on to become strong societies that exert cultural and economic influence on the rest of the world. This is certain evidence that progress and prosperity— let alone survival—do not depend on military victory.

"Bystander" nations fare well, too. Small neutral states like Switzerland, or states like Poland that are politically controlled by others, manage to survive both physically and culturally. They are even respected for their economic prosperity or for the personal courage of their citizens.

We can, if we choose, reject "fight-or-die" thinking. We can learn to deal with our personal anger and fear in ways other than war. Indeed, we may make unexpected gains from abandoning the habit of projection. If we cease using the enemy as a scapegoat, we might be more willing to look at, and deal creatively with, the serious problems and cruelties of our own systems. Humankind, after all, has an enormous capacity to learn and invent.

Chapter Eight

The Terror of "Little Wars"

On the afternoon of September 30, 1956, two bombs exploded at almost the same time in the French quarter of Algiers, a beautiful city on the coast of North Africa. One went off at the Milk-Bar, a soda fountain full of European children and mothers returning from a day at the beach. The second blew apart the Cafeteria, a popular hangout for European teenagers. A third bomb, planted at the air terminal, failed to explode. All together there were three deaths and over fifty serious injuries— including a dozen amputated limbs.

This was the first in a series of bombings and assassinations that would rock Algiers for over a year. Europeans living in the area were shocked, as were officials of the ruling French government. The unknown bombers were denouncd as criminals, fanatics, psychopaths.

Special military police were rushed to the city and given unlimited power to discover and crush the "terrorist" organization responsible.

People all over the world, especially within the last decade, have become aware of and frightened by such acts of seemingly random violence. Ships are hijacked and vacationing passengers killed in the Mediterranean; black policemen are shot dead in South Africa; American nuns are captured, raped and then killed by government troops in El Salvador. Bombs are exploded in a crowded department store in Paris, at a discotheque in Berlin, at an airport in Rome. And, as the technology of explosives has become increasingly sophisticated, more and more bystanders have been killed.

Bombings, kidnappings, murders--these are illegal indiscriminate attacks on peaceful civilians and government officials. What do they have to do with war? War is an organized, socially approved activity. It follows certain clear rules and regulations. Surely the terrorists who killed innocent women and children in Algiers were not soldiers. In that case, didn't their actions make them criminals?

We now know the names and motives of the young Algerian men who in 1956 worked in secret places in the native quarter—the Casbah—and built the bombs. We also know the names and motives of the young Algerian women who dressed themselves in European-style clothing and delivered the bombs. (At the time, of course, these men and women kept secret their identities and the names of others in the group.)

They were members of the National Liberation Front of Algeria, which had been outlawed by the French-controlled government. These people saw themselves as soldiers in an underground army—not criminals, but "freedom fighters." Since 1953 they had been fighting to end a century of French rule. They wanted an independent, Islamic, socialist republic, and they continued their fight until, in 1962, they achieved their goal.

During the early years of the National Liberation Army, its members kept to the sparsely settled, mountainous countryside. There they recruited small bands of farmers and craftsmen, staged attacks on the French army and police force and terrorized local European landowners and Muslims who were cooperating with the French. Attacks on the French barracks and police stations were particularly important, since this was the Liberation Army's main way of obtaining weapons.

These rural military operations continued even as a terrorist campaign was carried out in Algiers. In March 1957, for example, a commando unit led by Si Azedine—a man who had once been a coppersmith—ambushed a French army unit. Azedine's forces killed sixty of the French soldiers, with a loss of only seven rebel lives. The rebels ended the fighting when French aircraft appeared, and then spent a month hiding in the mountains or dispersed among their native villages. Then, in April, they ambushed a battalion of riflemen, killing ten including the captain.

In May of that same year, three hundred of Azedine's commandos were themselves ambushed by several com-

panies of French paratroopers. Three days of hard fighting followed before the Algerians could escape, carrying
with them their wounded and the weapons of their dead.
Ninety-six were killed and nine had been taken prisoner,
while among the French only eight men were dead and
twenty-nine wounded. But the French could not consider this battle a victory. The main body of the rebels
had survived—to recruit others and continue fighting.[1]

The tactics used by the Algerian National Liberation
Front, including both hit-and-run military ambushes and
terrorist violence, are associated with a very particular
kind of war: guerrilla warfare.

The word "guerrilla" is Spanish, and means "little
war." First used in the early nineteenth century during
Napoleon's attempt to conquer Spain, the word referred
to the irregular fighting carried on by Spanish people—
peasants, priests and aristocrats—who for a variety of
reasons resisted him. (The priests and aristocrats feared
the liberal political changes he would introduce. The
peasants feared and hated his army, which, by deliberate
policy lived off the land.) Guerrilla has since come to
be used as a label for any war in which the weak attempt
to oppose the strong through harassment and surprise,
while minimizing or evading direct military confron-
tations.

Guerrilla warfare is waged against those who have
won traditional wars of greed; it also opposes hierarchical, authoritarian states. It is by no means a new form
of warfare. Slaves have revolted against their lack of
freedom, peasants against an increase in taxes and reli-

gious minorities against persecution. Tribal groups resisted conquest by the Roman Empire; French and Yugoslav patriots resisted Nazi conquest of their countries.[2]

The Bible, like all ancient histories, is full of guerrilla operations. The First Book of Samuel tells that when David was outlawed by King Saul, he escaped to the Cave of Adullam. There he raised a small army and, over the next few years, harassed Saul—in typical guerrilla fashion. David's ragged soldiers fought when they felt they could win and temporarily disbanded at other times, scattering over the countryside and blending in with ordinary farmers and herdsmen. The men and women who joined David were described as "oppressed, in debt and discontented."[3] David, like many guerrilla leaders before and since, made himself the spokesman for economically exploited people.

Later Jewish leaders made themselves the spokesmen for a different but equally common kind of discontent: a religiously motivated rebellion.

In Palestine, for example, the Maccabees won liberation from Graeco-Syrian rulers in 158 B.C. They had begun their operations nine years earlier with an act of terrorism, when Matthias Maccabeus killed a priest officiating at a ceremony that was—in his view—"pagan." Matthias's son, Judah, continued the rebellion in typical guerrilla fashion. As the Second Book of Maccabees explains, he often swept down on a "pagan" village or town to burn it, or put Graeco-Syrian troops to rout in an ambush. These forays, for the most part carried out at nighttime, continued "till the fame of his valour spread far and wide."[4]

Guerrilla operations based upon religious hostility are characteristic of the monotheistic religions—Judaism, Christianity and Islam. The belief in a single deity and the claim of exclusive, correct insight into the way he must be worshipped seems often to have produced an intolerance for other religious beliefs and believers. For example, such intolerance was the source of the Catholic-Protestant conflict that created devastating civil wars in France in the sixteenth century; the same kind of conflict continues to devastate Northern Ireland today. It also fuels the complex guerrilla operations of the modern Near East, where Muslims attack non-Muslims and at the same time fight with each other over the validity of a Sunni or Shiite approach to the teachings of Islam.

Americans have also employed guerrilla tactics, rebelling (like the Algerians) against foreign colonial rule. The Boston Tea Party, praised in our history books as an action of patriots and the symbolic beginning of our independence from England, was an act of terrorism. Masked rebels illegally boarded an English ship and destroyed privately owned tea on which merchants had— in obedience to the law—paid import taxes.

It was, of course, relatively mild; property was attacked, not human beings. But it was intended to strike terror into the hearts of English loyalists, causing them to fear for their lives as well as their tea.

The history of the United States also glorifies the "midnight ride of Paul Revere" and the farmers who fought and defeated the British army at Concord. These farmers were guerrilla fighters. They responded to a secret call to arms and ambushed a legitimate army. The American guerrillas, after their initial success, went back into hiding. They returned to their farms and villages, where they were indistinguishable from peaceful civilians. The British government, quite naturally, considered them outlaws and traitors.

Though guerrilla operations have a long history, they have become much more common and successful since the industrial revolution. Alexander, for example, didn't have to worry about whether ordinary men and women would consent to his rule. Peasants armed with hoes, rakes and pitchforks, or tribal warriors armed with arrows and lances, could mount an ambush, but they could not inflict much damage on his soldiers, who were protected by iron shields, helmets and breastplates.

Modern peasants armed with rifles and grenades—or machine guns and howitzers—are much more dangerous. A carefully organized ambush can be expected to wipe out a platoon—or severely maul a brigade. Moreover, modern armies, unlike Alexander's soldiers, who carried their food and weapons on their backs, require a continuous supply of food, fuel and ammunition if they are to be efficient. And these supplies are very vulnerable: bridges and roads can be blown up and convoys can easily be hijacked.

As a result, guerrilla armies are much more difficult to "pacify." The French fought to control Algeria for almost ten years before abandoning the war. The Soviet attempts to eliminate Afghanistan guerrillas have been just as lengthy and—to date—just as unsuccessful.[5]

Established states, when confronted with rebellion, will deny the legitimacy of guerrilla operations directed against their right to rule. They will mobilize their armies to counter the guerrilla attack and treat captured rebels as civilians who have committed crimes rather than as soldiers who are prisoners of war. Other countries, who are allies of such governments, will adopt the same attitude and support attempts to eliminate the "uncivilized" or "criminal" behavior. During the American Revolution Hessian troops from Germany aided the British in their efforts against the American colonists. In the 1960s the United States aided the counterguerrilla efforts of the South Vietnamese government.[6]

Rulers may deny the legitimacy of rebels, but this denial of legitimacy also works the other way. Rebels decry their rulers and the aid these rulers may receive from foreign states. Rebels may argue, often with the backing of respected political philosophers and religious leaders, that the existing state—and its allies—are unjust, pagan, heretical, capitalist, imperialist, atheistic or communistic. Like the established governments, they insist that *their* side is in the right. And they try to gain recognition of *their* legitimacy, as well as material aid from their less politically active countrymen and from foreign governments.

Guerrilla wars often become deeply intertwined with more conventional international conflict. David, the rebel leader, was aided by the Philistines, who wished to undermine the strength of Israel. American revolutionaries were supported by the French monarchy, which considered England its traditional enemy. And the Algerians were given arms and money by Tunisia, Yugoslavia and other countries intent on reducing the power of European, American and Russian "imperialists."

Those who support terrorists and guerrillas in other countries do not necessarily tolerate similar attempts to overthrow their own regimes. But decisions to support—or ignore—revolutionaries in other countries seem to have little to do with the legitimacy of the guerrilla cause—assuming that can be determined. These decisions are, instead, linked to supposed national interests. Thus the Russians are currently engaged in a long-drawn-out war against Islamic guerrillas challenging a Marxist regime they support in Afghanistan. At the same time, they are sympathetic to, and supportive of, the equally Islamic Palestinian guerrilla movement. Similarly, the United States has been hostile to and horrified by guerrilla operations in El Salvador, while providing the primary support for *contra* guerrillas (praising them as "freedom fighters") in Nicaragua.

In truth, "de-legitimization"—a form of political propaganda declaring the actions of a particular group unwarranted—is one of the tactics used in a guerrilla war by both established governments and rebels. However, once a guerrilla operation succeeds, its legitimacy will be recognized by everyone. The new leaders of a country will participate in the peace conference that ends the war. They will be accorded international recognition, the equality and dignity of a sovereign nation. A very high percentage of the states that are now members of the United Nations achieved their present status at least partially through guerrilla activities. This includes almost all the states in the Western hemisphere and at least half of those in Africa and Asia!

People who were once successful guerrilla leaders—King David, Paul Revere, Mao Ze-dong—are remembered and honored in the histories of their nations as "founding fathers." History books legitimize their violent rebellion and provide models for future guerrilla leaders. Indeed, praise in history books is the final step in social approval. Such approval, while it may be denied to any specific attempt at rebellion, is in the long run necessary to the success of guerrilla warfare.[7]

While a guerrilla war is being fought, however, both sides will refuse to acknowledge the legitimacy of the opposition's demands and activities. These are wars in which there are no rules. Indiscriminate violence is intensified because both sides desperately need the support of the people for their violence and counterviolence. And they need, as well, the approval of international public opinion.

Guerrilla leaders must create widespread sympathy and support for their actions. They will be dependent, after all, on ordinary citizens for food, shelter, protection and a continuous supply of fighting recruits for a long time, perhaps five to twenty years. The civilians themselves will often be hard-pressed just to survive. Guerrilla leaders also need foreign alliances and foreign aid.

Winning the "hearts and minds" of ordinary people thus becomes one of the real goals of a guerrilla war. The first approach is to gain active loyalty through propaganda, ideological appeals or kindly treatment. Thus, in Algeria the National Liberation Front, in its drive for voluntary recruits and supporters, reminded the citizens of that country of the discrimination they currently suffered; the Front appealed to Islamic pride and promised a better future. The French government, on the other hand, instituted serious economic reforms in the countryside and offered protection to the loyalists. But governments and rebels alike may also resort to violence to frighten men and women into at least passive loyalty or neutrality. Rebels will plant bombs in department stores; government pilots will bomb "enemy" villages. Rebels will assassinate village leaders friendly to the government, while rulers will arrest, torture and execute any citizen suspected of rebellious tendencies.

Terrorist tactics are a part of the struggle for the attention and loyalty of the population as a whole. They are, in effect, theatrical events intended to dramatize the seriousness of the situation. The Algerian terrorists in 1956 were seeking to attract the attention of the international press in order to increase foreign support for the National Liberation Front.[8]

The scope of such terrorist operations has widened dramatically in recent years. Modern transportation and communication increase the ease of movement, while guerrilla and counterguerrilla activities have become international. Consider what happens when a democratically elected government such as the United States supports a regime, like Israel, that is under attack by guerrillas. The citizens of the U.S.—the foreign ally—become part of the "enemy resources" that the guerrillas feel they must influence—thus the taking of American hostages.

The actual effectiveness of such tactics is dubious. For example, the Provisional Irish Republican Army, known as the IRA, has been trying since the late 1960s to over-throw the Protestant-dominated government of Ulster in Northern Ireland. Since England supports the existing government in Ulster, the attitude of ordinary English people is a factor in the future of Ulster and is of concern to the IRA. They see English civilians as one of their targets. As a result, the IRA has assassinated revered English statesmen, like Lord Mountbatten, and planted bombs in English hotels and factories, in addition to harassing English troops in Northern Ireland. They hope to influence the policy of the English people and their government. But the English voting public has not yet refused to pay the economic and emotional cost of sup-porting the existing Ulster government.[9]

Guerrilla wars are very costly. Few of the individuals who initiated the Algerian rebellion survived to enjoy the benefits of independence. And the eight years of struggle were devastating: Over three quarters of a mil-lion (out of a total Islamic population of nine million) died in the process. Similar or larger losses accompanied successful guerrilla struggles in Yugoslavia, China and Vietnam.

What can lead men and women to undertake and per-
severe in such a costly and devastating war? And how
are those individuals who initiate resistance or rebellion
different from those who do not?

Their opponents say they are immature, unable to
adjust, psychopathic, unrealistic, addicted to violence.
Yet in many terrorist and guerrilla leaders who come to
power—David in Judah, Samuel Adams in the United
States, Houari Boumedienne in Algeria, Menachem Begin
in Israel, Josip Tito in Yugoslavia, for example—these
qualities are not evident. Rather, these men seemed to
be distinguished from other political leaders mainly by
their efficiency and a high level of self-confidence.

Not all guerrillas continue to be involved in military
or political activities once they have won. Paul Revere
went back to work as a silversmith. Saadi Yacef, who
directed the terrorist campaign in Algiers, became a very
successful movie producer. Zohra Drif, one of the women
who planted bombs for him, was later a lawyer and
secretary-general of the Algerian National School of
Administration. Another female terrorist became head
of the Algerian branch of Max Factor. These are not
professions associated with psychological disorders or
immaturity.

Nonetheless, most guerrilla leaders *are* impatient and
unwilling to adjust to the status quo.

What produces such rebellious men and women?

To understand them we must look at the ways people
are brought up in all societies. Parents rightly try to
train their children to survive and prosper, and so teach

techniques of *prudence*: how to get by, what rules must
be followed, what to avoid, when to obey those who
are powerful and authoritative.

Children also come to identify themselves with their
own group—be it their nation, social class, religion, race
or culture. They learn, for example, a language (like
English or Spanish), which is both a useful tool for
communication and a means of differentiating them from
those who do not speak that language. They see themselves as English- or Spanish-speaking. As they learn
the beauty of their language and the wonderful things
that other English or Spanish speakers have accomplished, they come to have a sense of self-esteem and
dignity.

Such group identity, if it fulfills one's needs and en-
hances one's sense of power, can create a very strong
group loyalty: It comes to seem the very "center of one's
being." Thus, older immigrants into the United States—
from Mexico or Italy or Thailand—may refuse to give
up their language and learn English despite the practical
handicaps such loyalty imposes on them. However, Jewish
immigrants fleeing Nazi Germany in the 1930s readily
abandoned German for obvious reasons, and learned
English with great rapidity.

Under ideal situations—when a person is a member
of a majority group in power, for example—prudence
and group loyalty work hand in hand, providing both
the survival techniques and the feeling of security needed
for a workable, productive life. But there are times when
prudence and loyalty come into conflict. At the moment

of a foreign conquest, or when a successful revolution—like the one in France in 1789—produces a radical change in the social and economic structure and even the culture of an existing state, within each individual and within the conquered group as a whole, there is very real psychological distress. A prudent person will want to obey the new rulers, but loyalty to the original group calls for resistance.

Young people from families that hold values different from the majority are often—in much smaller ways—faced with prudence/loyalty conflicts. Consider the plight of a girl from a very religious family with strict ideas about the way she should dress. Perhaps everyone she knows at school is wearing the makeup and trendy outfits that her parents consider improper. (A young person in Germany during the Nazi period might have found students wearing uniforms that her parents considered immoral.) The prudent—and easiest—way to gain acceptance at school will be to adopt her peers' style of dressing. But if she is to remain loyal to her parents and her church, she must continue to wear modest clothing and no makeup. (Or refuse to join a Nazi youth group and wear its uniform.) Like conquered people or minority groups throughout history, she will be caught between conflicting desires, pulled in different directions by prudence and loyalty.

For adults in the aftermath of conquest or revolution, prudence, or careful observance of the new rules of society, is the surest way of staying alive. Most individuals and groups will choose to obey and even cooperate with new rulers. This was true for the majority of individuals and nations conquered by the Nazis in World War II, as it was for most of the Algerians conquered by the French in 1847. It was also true for most of the aristocrats and church leaders who lost power and influence as a result of the French Revolution. Conquerors and successful revolutionaries count on such a prudent response to simplify their task of governing.

But some men and women resist conquest or a successful revolution. Like Tito and his Yugoslav followers resisting Nazi conquests, or the *contras*, who reject the Sandinista government in Nicaragua, they resort to guerrilla warfare. In effect, they resolve the conflict between prudence and loyalty in a different way. They feel so strongly tied to their group—defined by religion or nation or class—that their personal sense of self-esteem and self-worth is threatened by their group's defeat. Their own physical survival seems unimportant; they refuse to be prudent. Instead, they voluntarily risk their lives in an attempt to preserve independence or power or dignity for their group and for themselves.

When even guerrilla resistance fails, a person can remain loyal to the politically defeated group by quietly and privately continuing to follow the group's language, culture and religion—"internalized resistance." This was the response of the Jews after their second rebellion against the Roman Empire was crushed and the temple in Jerusalem destroyed. They accepted their political defeat but remained loyal to their religious heritage.

However, conquered ethnic and religious groups like

the Basques and the Irish Catholics, though ruled for centuries by Spain and Protestant England, respectively, maintained both prudence and an ongoing and resentful sense of "us" versus "them." The conflict they felt when first conquered was passed on to succeeding generations through customs, stories and songs. And it has been expressed from time to time in guerrilla operations.

Conquered people can also adapt and adjust to a new group loyalty by "assimilation." This path was followed by the elite of most of the populations conquered by Rome. Within a generation or two, they submerged older loyalties in a new pride in being Roman. In the same way, many of the upper-class people of India attempted during the nineteenth century to become British. They learned to speak English, wore European clothing and sent their children to school in England. The parents of Mahatma Gandhi did this.

In the Roman Empire, the process of assimilation was aided—and centuries of relative peace sustained—because the Romans offered citizenship to any educated or wealthy person who would serve them. The Romans also greatly admired some of the special skills and cultural achievements of the defeated people. But what the Romans did was unusual, and even they did not extend equality or dignity to religiously Orthodox Jews or to the lower classes.

All elites justify their right to conquer, tax and govern with claims of inherent superiority, "divine right" or "survival of the fittest." Class, caste, racial or religious differences are taken as evidence of the inferiority of the oppressed group. Even Aristotle, the great philosopher-teacher of ancient Athens, followed this course of thinking. He argued that barbarians and women were—unlike Greek males—biologically inferior and incapable of self-government.

The French adopted a similar attitude toward the Islamic Arabs in Algeria. Jules Roy, who was French but born and raised in Algeria, described his indoctrination into this way of thinking: "One thing I knew because it was told me so often, was that the Arabs belonged to a different race, one inferior to my own. . . . Yes, their happiness was elsewhere, rather, if you please, like the happiness of cattle. . . . I was glad to believe it. . . . Who suffers seeing oxen sleep on straw or eating grass?"[10]

When guerrillas rebel against a long-established government, their leaders may have had parents who were either internal resisters or assimilationists. Houari Boumedienne, who has been president of independent Algeria for over twenty years, was the son of a strict Muslim farmer who spoke no French. Houari himself was a student at the Arab-Islamic school in Constantine, Algeria, and at El Azhar University in Cairo—both centers of anti-Western, Islamic fundamentalist thought. But most of the founders of the Algerian National Liberation Front were initially assimilationists: They had served as noncommissioned officers in the French army during World War II and were unusual among Arabs for their command of the French language. Ho Chi Minh, leader of the Vietnamese guerrillas, was fluent in French and English and had spent many years in Europe.

These people abandoned the assimilation attempted by their parents. They learned through bitter experience that they—or the values with which they identified—would never truly be accepted by the ruling group. They would always be considered inferior. France refused in the late 1940s to make even minor reforms in its governing of Algeria—and this was after two decades of peaceful Algerian agitation, and substantial military contributions by Algerians to the cause of "free France" during World War II. For Ho Chi Minh the turning point was the Versailles Peace Conference at the end of World War I. He had believed in the victorious Allies' wartime promises to redraw state boundaries on the basis of "self-determination." So he rented formal Western clothes and traveled to Paris to plead for Indochina's independence. The Allied leaders refused to even listen to his arguments.[11]

When a person offers loyalty and is rejected, the implication is that the person himself has no value. This can be psychologically intolerable.

Consider a student who wants to be part of the dominant group at school, and who does everything he can to please its leaders, but who is rejected and ridiculed. We have all seen this happen. Perhaps the student wears the wrong kind of clothes, or is too bookish or clumsy, or is a member of the "wrong" minority group. A person who is rejected in this way, after having made the effort to be "prudent" and adopt the values of the majority, feels degraded and *very angry*.

Rather than acknowledge such a loss of esteem, young

people may turn their anger on themselves, often responding to such treatment by clowning, or withdrawing, or engaging in antisocial acts, such as drug use. Future guerrilla leaders, having been treated this way, will set out to seek independence and dignity—for their people and for themselves. Impatience born of frustrated hopes and rage born of injured pride can make violence seem a powerful and necessary choice.

The experience of a black South African mother helps us understand what can happen at such times. Speaking in July 1986 to the World Methodist Conference in Nairobi, Kenya, she talked about the one brief visit she was allowed with her imprisoned daughter. At that time the young woman had been in solitary confinement for over six months, as punishment for having participated in an antiapartheid demonstration. The mother reported that she was terrified by the fury she perceived in her child, and in other young black South Africans.

Commenting on her talk, the Reverend John V. Moore, one of the American delegates to the conference, reflected, "Rage conceived in injustice and born in oppression is a gift of God. But it is a gift mixed with terror . . . [which] can consume those in whom it dwells, as well as those who provoke it."[12]

The word "provoke" is critical.

The provocation comes from ruling governments and elites who refuse to adopt democratic measures or recognize the humanity and value of the governed. Indeed, the only lasting and effective response to guerrilla warfare seems to be the adoption by the establishment of liberal, representative ways of governing. (Of course, authoritarian police states can, for a while, repress most forms of dissent. But the current and massive stirrings of dissidence and even rebellion in China, South Korea and the border republics of the Soviet Union make it clear that such repression does not work forever.)[13]

Representative government will not eliminate individual attempts to provoke change through violence, but it will eliminate popular support for such activities. Thus, in the 1960s, when discontented groups tried to initiate urban guerrilla warfare in Uruguay, the democratic government of that country waited until it was certain that popular sentiment had turned against the violence of the rebels. It then used its police force to arrest and convict the isolated—and therefore powerless—guerrillas.[14] As long as peaceful change seems possible, most people will prefer to avoid the dangers of civil warfare.

Unfortunately, truly democratic political structures are still rare. And we have no international government capable of providing a peaceful means for change. Governments that are rigid and willing to use violence to sustain a status quo evoke "rage conceived in injustice." People who are thwarted in their attempts to secure change peacefully and punished for their efforts will experience that rage, and they are likely to turn to guerrilla techniques. They will call on others to join them in rebellion. As a result, in the words of Reverend Moore, "the grapes of wrath are stored in South Africa [and every oppressive state] . . . where the violence of the

South African government can only ignite a counter-violence."[15]

However, a violent response is not the only option.

One of the most significant changes in recent American history—the desegregation of public facilities in the South—was brought about through nonviolent means. The first step in the process involved several decades of legal action, which finally bore fruit in 1954 when the United States Supreme Court declared segregation in the schools illegal. But the Supreme Court decision did not even touch the other forms of segregation created by "Jim Crow" laws, which separated whites and "coloreds" in restaurants, rest rooms, hospital wards, swimming pools and a host of other public accommodations.

Since blacks were routinely denied the right to register and vote in the Southern states, these laws could not be overturned by the ballot box. If each form of segregation had to be tackled by long litigation like that which had preceded that 1954 decision, getting them all declared illegal would take at least another century. Moreover, many southern governors—like Faubus in Arkansas and Wallace in Georgia—were refusing to obey the Supreme Court and daring the reluctant federal government to intervene with force in this issue of "states' rights."

Then on December 1, 1955, in Montgomery, Alabama, Rosa Parks made her now-famous decision not to yield her seat on a municipal bus to a white man. At that time Southern city ordinances required segregation on buses. Blacks were restricted to the back of the bus, but when buses became crowded, the white seating area was expanded toward the back—and blacks were required to give up their seats. They had to stand in the rear. Rosa Parks's refusal to give up her seat was, in fact, illegal.

Rosa Parks's decision was not made on the spur of the moment, or simply because she was tired. She worked as a seamstress, but also had been the secretary of the local chapter of the National Association for the Advancement of Colored People. She was quite aware of a previous test of the segregation of Montgomery's buses: In 1954 a high-school sophomore, Claudette Colvin, had been arrested for refusing to obey the law requiring that she surrender her seat. Colvin had been given a suspended sentence, and the Montgomery City Commission and the bus company had promised changes. But no change had been forthcoming.

Blacks in Montgomery, in a meeting the following night, decided to embark on a policy of nonviolent resistance. They set aside Monday, December 5, 1955, as a day to boycott the buses. The weekend was spent organizing and telephoning, getting out hurriedly printed notices and attempting to organize car pools. And on Monday morning, as the boycott leaders—including Martin Luther King, Jr.—anxiously watched, the boycott proved to be a success. Near-empty buses maneuvered through streets crowded with blacks walking to work, as 90 percent of Montgomery's black population refused to ride on segregated buses.

While they were breaking no laws, they had chosen a course of action as dangerous as it was difficult. The boycott continued, eventually lasting an entire year. White segregationist leaders denounced the boycott, and blamed it on outside agitators and Communists. The patiently walking boycotters were subjected to ridicule and jeers. Violence soon followed. On January 10, 1956, four black churches were bombed. Ministers' homes were bombed—King's three times.

Still, the thousands of individual heroes of the black community persisted in their peaceful boycott. Calm and courageous, with no end to their struggle in sight, they persisted in the difficult course they had chosen. And they persisted, as well, in refusing to respond in kind to hate and violence.[16]

"In our protest there will be no cross burnings," Martin Luther King, Jr., declared from the pulpit at the outset of the boycott. "No white person will be taken from his home by a hooded Negro mob and brutally murdered. There will be no threats and intimidation."[17]

Eventually the enormous sacrifices of Montgomery's black community were rewarded. On December 20, 1956, the segregationists and the bus company at last gave in. The buses were desegregated. Moreover, nonviolent opposition had been established within the black community as a viable means of achieving desegregation and justice. Over the next ten years, nonviolent sit-ins, "freedom rides" and massive marches were mounted in one southern community after another and in Washington, D.C. They forced changes in public policy directly in many Southern communities—and they created a national sentiment that made possible federal legislation outlawing racial discrimination and insuring the vote.

Mahatma Gandhi, Martin Luther King, Jr., and their followers used a nonviolent—but still rebellious—response to oppression. Gandhi and King were as convinced as any guerrilla fighter that the conditions of British rule in India or discriminatory segregation in America were wrong. They were also convinced that the oppressed had a moral obligation to resist exploitation and humiliation. Gandhi and King knew their resistance to oppression would be costly, that their followers would be attacked, jailed, beaten and even killed. In fact, both Gandhi and King were themselves assassinated. But they asked men and women to put aside the constraints of prudence out of loyalty to the group. They asked them to demand recognition for the dignity and rights of their people.[18]

Gandhi and King combined their fervent resistance to oppression with an equally fierce concern for all of humanity. They refused to limit their loyalty to a single group. Instead, they affirmed that every individual, however mistaken or evil in his or her acts, was a fellow human being and worthy of love. They believed group loyalty should carry with it a larger loyalty to the human group as a whole. In King's words, "Love must be our ideal. Love your enemies, bless them, and pray for them. Let no man pull you so low as to make you hate him."[19]

Both Gandhi and King spoke in religious terms, but

United by their belief in equality and nonviolence, hundreds of thousands of Americans came to Washington, D.C., in 1963 to urge the passage of civil rights legislation. (following pages)   UPI/Bettmann Newsphotos

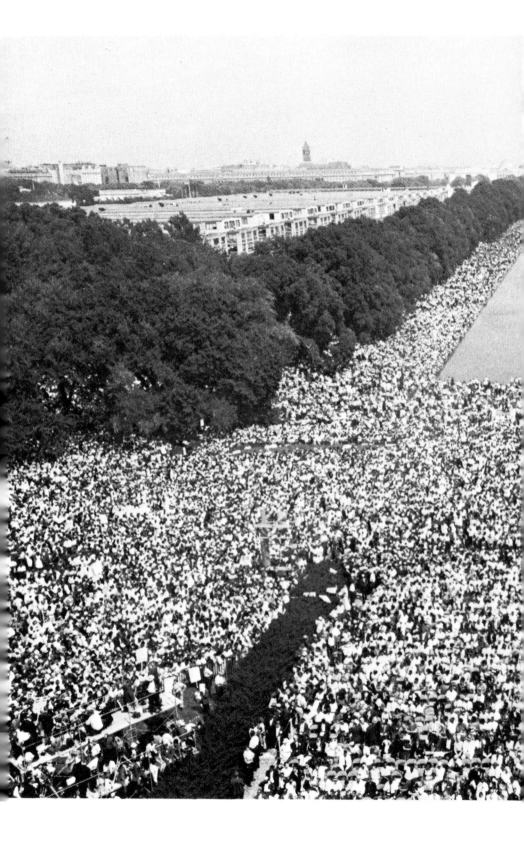

their message makes sense in psychological terms as well.

The person we would see as "the other," different from ourselves, the one who wears the black hat in the "good guy/bad guy" myth, is not as different from us as we would like to think. Instead, like "the enemy" of neolithic people, he is a projection. Like the German poster designer or President Roosevelt in World War II, we attribute to "the other" the parts of ourselves we don't like or are reluctant to face.

Such projection results in prejudice and stereotyping. We decide in advance that everyone who wears a black hat is a "bad guy" because we have projected negative qualities onto the black-hat group. We also assume that all members of the white-hat group are, like us, "good guys." King and Gandhi, however, saw clearly that we are all part of a larger group: the human race.

Some people are so filled with unacknowledged self-hate that their projections become especially negative, and their responses to what they perceive as otherness are violent. They want to eliminate the "bad" parts of themselves they have projected onto others. Thus, in attempting to punish or eliminate the "bad guy," many of us, like our Neolithic ancestors, are unconsciously trying to eliminate the "bad" parts of ourselves.

Economic or religious oppression comes from a misguided search by the oppressor for approval and self-esteem—as when the French attempted to assure themselves that they were indeed better than the lazy, immoral, misguided Algerians. The other side of that coin

is the violent rebellious rage of the oppressed, which ultimately grows out of a desire for approval and dignity.

Whether we seek to deny the humanity of the oppressed or attempt to eradicate the oppressor, we are at
the same time denying and attempting to destroy part
of our own selves, the part that is either identified with
(projected onto) or attracted to the "other."

Religious fanaticism, in particular, which condemns
and wishes to destroy a different religious group, has
its psychological roots in the attractiveness of the other
religion, which is denied by the fanatic. At first glance,
the fanatic seems to have no self-doubts, to be rigidly
and unalterably opposed to other religions and convinced of the rightness of his own beliefs. For example,
when in 1095 Pope Urban II attacked the Muslims as
"this vile race," "so despised, degenerate, and slave of
the demons," he seemed to be—like all fanatics in their
public guise—totally sure of himself and the correctness
of his position. And of course that is the self-image the
fanatic wishes to preserve.

But in attacking the Muslims, Urban found it necessary to deny that Islam shares with Christianity "faith
in an omnipotent God." He also found it necessary to
forget that Jesus had clearly said, "Blessed are the peace-
makers," or that it was Mohammed, not Jesus, who had
taught that "holy wars" against the infidel were legitimate. Instead Urban invented a command from Christ
(who lived six hundred years before Mohammed) requiring his followers to "eliminate these idolaters."[20] (A
strange term, incidentally, for members of a religion

that is even more opposed than Christianity or Judaism to any potentially idolatrous representation of living beings.)

Urban's distortions of reality—and the failure of his audience to notice them—were not just accidents. Rather, they are part of an unconscious denial that a monotheistic and war-glorifying religion different from his own might in any way be attractive to him and the warlike nobility of medieval Christianity.

The example of Urban also points to another tendency: Violent fanaticism is particularly likely to erupt between religious groups that are rather similar, like the monotheistic religions that share a common origin in Judaism. A religion totally different from one's own normally arouses amusement or curiosity, not desire or attraction. One can be tolerant because it creates no anxious doubts about the solidity of one's own religious faith.

Attraction and doubt, consciously denied but unconsciously very potent, threaten the self-image (and the possible salvation) of the fanatic who attempts to "purify" him- or herself by purifying the world. If one cannot entirely eliminate one's own desires, one can at least eliminate the external object of those desires. In the words of Paul Tillich, a famous Protestant theologian, the fanatic—whether a Protestant, a Shiite or an Orthodox Jew—demonstrates by the violence of his disagreement the "elements in [his] spiritual life . . . which he must suppress in himself."[21]

Similarly, the hostility frequently expressed against

homosexuals often emerges in its most vicious form among people who feel threatened by their own feelings—especially men who fear and wish to deny that they themselves have ever had any sexual urges that weren't absolutely "straight." It is often the most obviously "masculine" male who talks and makes jokes about searching out homosexuals and engaging in "queer bashing." The question of whether homosexual acts are immoral is not at issue here, but rather the ferocity with which some people, fearful of their own feelings, condemn homosexuality.

As long as we are unwilling to tolerate and accept parts of our own personalities, we will be unwilling to tolerate and accept the "others." This is true not only for personal relationships but also for international relations and guerrilla warfare. For this reason, successful guerrillas often create regimes just as oppressive and rigid—though in different ways—as the regimes they replace.

Gandhi and King did not engage in projection. They had the courage to accept their own weaknesses and acknowledge the goodness in their enemies. They recognized that as human beings we are all a mixture of strength and weakness, love and hate. Because they accepted themselves, they could accept others. Instead of believing the "good guy/bad guy" myth, they saw that each person has a good and a bad guy inside him. Gandhi and King had no "enemies," no "other." Or, in the words of the comic-strip character Pogo, "We have met the enemy and he is us."

Nonviolent resistance is different from guerrilla resistance because it deliberately refuses to engage in projection. Instead, it insists on the full humanity of the oppressed and simultaneously recognizes the humanity of the oppressor. It demands tolerance of the complex blend of good and bad that is part of any individual or group. Gandhi made this clear when he deliberately adopted an Englishwoman as his daughter. Similarly, King worked closely with white friends and encouraged white participation in the civil rights movement.

Gandhi and King believed that a loving and suffering resistance to evil *acts* (rather than evil *people*) offered the possibility for new and creative ways to resolve conflicts. Indeed, their approach can lead to a mutual recognition of a shared humanity, and the basis for a "beloved community" of all mankind.[22]

Still, for most people, resorting to violence as a means of solving problems seems to have more appeal than using nonviolent resistance. That is understandable. Although it seems at first glance that warrior heroes are courageous, the truth is that nonviolent resistance requires much more inner strength.

Resorting to violence is easier, because it allows people to avoid two kinds of risks.

First is the risk of accepting those parts of themselves that they might prefer to project onto the enemy. Violence allows us to deny the humanity of the "other." Therefore, the situation is "us" versus "them," and we can continue to believe that we are totally good and they are totally evil. We don't have to find within ourselves courage to face the mixture of good and bad that is part of us—and of all humankind.

The second risk of nonviolence is the need to take action. Nonviolent resistance, to be successful, depends on the voluntary actions—the courage, patience and sacrifice—of hundreds and thousands of ordinary men and women. It requires unified action by the oppressed. Men, women and children must all find within themselves the courage to risk danger, loneliness and absurdity. During India's struggle for independence and during the civil rights struggle in the United States, thousands of people showed a willingness to fill the jails, and accepted the possibility of being beaten and even killed. They did this because they knew this is the only way nonviolent resistance will work. On the other hand, resistance through violence allows the bulk of a population to remain prudently passive, delegating the risks of conflict—and therefore the need for courage—onto a smaller and self-selected group of fighters.

Nonviolent resistance depends not on a few brilliant warrior heroes but on the empowering heroism of everyone. Unfortunately, most people do not yet believe in nonviolent resistance as a means of securing justice.

Chapter Nine

Building the Ramparts of Peace

"It may seem melodramatic to say that the United States and Russia represent Good and Evil. But if we think of it that way, it helps to clarify our perspective on the world struggle."[1] These are the words of Richard Nixon, spoken when he was president in the 1960s. Other political leaders, often with less self-awareness, fall into the trap of the "good guy/bad guy" simplification. In the 1960s, for example, Ian Paisley, leader of the militant Protestant Ulster Democratic Unionist Party, was convinced that any priest was an "idolatrous Mass-mongering representative of the Papal Antichrist."[2]

And in the same period, Chinese leaders were attacking the U.S.S.R. for "allying with the forces of war to oppose the forces of peace, allying with imperialism to oppose socialism . . . and allying with the reactionaries of all countries to oppose the people of the world."[3] The Russians, in reply, accused the Chinese of taking a position "close in many respects to that of the 'madmen'— the representatives of the extremely aggressive imperialist circles."[4] Each of the two countries, moreover, accused the other of harboring "racist" sentiments!

Sam Keen, in his book *Faces of the Enemy*, points out the mutual nature of this kind of name-calling. "Clearly Soviet propaganda picturing the United States as an abuser of civil rights is the pot calling the kettle black. And just as clearly, our tirades against Soviet state control . . . reflect an unconscious anger at the real loss of individual freedom under corporate capitalism, and our dependence on the government."[5]

The thin line between anger at our own society and anger directed against the enemy is quite obvious in Sylvester Stallone's *Rambo* films. The enemies in *Rambo I: "First Blood"* are American policemen, National Guardsmen and a small civilian village. The enemy in *Rambo II* is represented by both Vietnamese soldiers and American military technocrats. Rambo is driven by enormous and relatively unfocused rage; he can discover an enemy almost anywhere.

Similarly, hostile energy is targeted on Darth Vader in the *Star Wars* films and on a host of galactic villains in the *Star Trek* stories. The same pattern exists in earlier films, in which a succession of macho heroes stride through the battlefields of World War II and the landscapes of the Old West.

Adventure stories that retell the "good guy/bad guy"

myth encourage us to understand relations between people and between countries in overly simple terms. As we have pointed out, "good guy/bad guy" thinking allows us to believe that we are good and the enemy is bad, and so project our own "undesirable" qualities onto our enemies. The myth also suggests that our enemies freely choose an evil course of action, but we—believing ourselves to be more or less on Death Ground—have no choice but to respond with violence.

This dangerous myth is one way of understanding the world, but it is by no means the only way. As human circumstances have changed throughout thousands of centuries, so have human beliefs and behavior. Our ideas about warfare today are a mixture of elements from the past.

We have held on to the neolithic idea that the enemy is evil, but have abandoned the idea that a way of life created "in the beginning" will never change. We continue to feel that greed is natural, even though warfare has largely been replaced by other means as a way of acquiring wealth. As in the days of Homer, we still want to have heroes, but unlike Homer, we now feel that our heroes—the "good guys"—must always win. Also, while we have given up nineteenth-century confidence in warfare as a way to achieve progress, many people still believe that preparedness for war will assure peace.

Despite the many elements added to or subtracted from our beliefs, our ideas about war still do not match reality. Our leaders, fearful of annihilation, cling to the peace-through-strength convictions of Tōgō Heihachirō and Theodore Roosevelt, even though this kind of thinking led to the frightful destruction of World Wars I and II.

Continually expanding arsenals bring about ever-increasing financial costs. Former U.S. Budget Director David Stockman calculated that by 1989—the end of the two-term Reagan presidency, during which an enormous arms buildup occurred—"the next president will inherit a publicly held debt nearly triple that accumulated by all of Ronald Reagan's 39 predecessors."[6] And a study conducted in 1986 at the University of California concluded that the cost of "Star Wars," or Strategic Defense Initiative, would triple in five years, requiring an outlay of $8.1 billion in 1991. The researchers also noted that in the four years just before they made their study, the federal government's support of military research had increased 50 percent, with an enormous loss to non-military research.[7]

Wars have always been costly. The people of Neolithic tribes had to abandon much of their regular work in order to do battle. Kings like Alexander and heroes like Achilles pursued their greed or their searches for glorious immortality while ignoring the costs to themselves and to ordinary people.

In more recent times, national leaders have waged war or insisted on being prepared to do so. And they have behaved as if the costs—in money, human lives and the quality of our natural environment—were relatively unimportant. Such thinking is not in keeping with reality.

Our leaders deny reality in another way as well. They

continue to prepare for a major world confrontation, yet other events seem far more likely. In recent decades international conflict has most often been carried out through "limited wars," such as the events in the Falkland Islands and Grenada, and continuing guerrilla and terrorist operations. The effectiveness of massive armed intervention by major powers in these situations is doubtful. Is the use of a fleet of battleships—or missiles—really appropriate in response to a takeover attempt in a small country or the hijacking of an airliner? At a minimum, as author Milton Meltzer observes: "To use threats and armed force instead of diplomacy and peaceful negotiation is to turn minor problems into colossal defeats."[8] And it perpetuates the world's commitment to military might as the solution to all problems.

Preparedness for an all-out global war is a denial of the most threatening reality: the extinction of human life. People who support the development of great nuclear arsenals don't accept the possibility that these weapons may be used. They don't actually expect *they* will be dead. They tell themselves the bombs will land elsewhere . . . or they will manage to escape the radioactive area in time . . . or there will be no devastating epidemics or lawlessness or famines . . . or there will still be drinkable water and air that is safe to breathe. Belief in the "good guy/bad guy" myth—by ordinary citizens and national leaders alike—underlies this enormous denial of reality.

Young people live in a world created, and largely dominated, by adults. Does that mean young people are powerless? Are they, like the people of Neolithic times, living in a world they do not understand and therefore cannot genuinely control?

No.

People, young and old, can—and do—create change. For example, in just the past decade or two, the fairy-tale myth of the sleeping princess waiting for her prince to awaken her has lost much of its power as girls and women have achieved independence and self-esteem on their own. And parents no longer believe in the old motto advocating corporal punishment: Spare the rod and spoil the child.

Such changes do not come about merely because of the passage of time; something *causes* the change. Women activists in the last few decades spoke up about the dire consequences—for men and women—of believing in the sleeping-princess "myth." People concerned with the welfare of children worked to help parents understand that there are better ways of dealing with their youngsters than beating them.

Change begins with understanding. If we understand the pitfalls of believing in the "good guy/bad guy" myth, we can refuse to accept what it teaches.

We know that the "good guy/bad guy" myth requires "enemies" on whom our own shortcomings may be projected. But we do not live in a black-and-white world in which our enemies are all bad and we are all good; in which our enemies choose an evil course of action and we have no choice but to respond with violence. Therefore, as individuals we must have the courage to admit our own weaknesses and to see in others good points as well as bad.

We know that the "good guy/bad guy" myth, in addition to calling for "enemies," calls for delegating to heroes the need for courage. In order to change, we must instead individually exercise courage in little ways, every day.

Finding courage may be particularly difficult for young people who have to deal with peer pressure and their own need for approval and acceptance. Taking a position that risks the approval of your friends or the people you admire can be frightening. People who do so risk being ostracized and ridiculed. They may face loneliness and isolation at a time in their lives when they most need the support of their friends. They may risk a loss of status and popularity. By advocating an unpopular cause, a young person takes on the same psychological risks as a civil rights marcher or advocate of passive resistance. It takes real courage to confront these painful circumstances at any time in one's life, in any context. But if every person, including our world leaders, practiced moral courage on a daily basis, the larger issues of human rights and world peace might be within our grasp.

Young people can involve themselves in the adult world. Young people and adults are not, after all, separate species who live in separate environments. Young people can share their understanding of the nature of war, and can argue the false vision of the world presented in the "good guy/bad guy" myth.

In the United States—a democratic society—leaders

are elected by a minority of the people. A passive majority does not vote, or remains so uninformed as to make an intelligent voting decision impossible. And it is a passive majority, as well, that allows the preparations for war to continue, along with exploitation, injustice and damage to the economy and the environment.

People seldom behave in passive ways because they genuinely don't care. Passivity—or ignorance of events—usually stems from an attitude that the actions of one person, or of a few, can make little difference. But Rosa Parks and the thousands of others who helped end segregation in Montgomery, Alabama, didn't feel this way. We must participate in our democracy and not delude ourselves that we can delegate our responsibilities for participation and courage to "heroes."

We must work to understand current events, and the attitudes and actions of our leaders. Do they tell us our problems can be blamed entirely on others? Do they speak out of insecurity and fear, urging the use of force against "enemies" within and outside of our own community or nation? Do they ignore or deny the terrible costs of armed conflict and urge the use of violence in response to problems?

Understanding—of events of the past as well as of today's history in the making—is essential to human survival. As has so often been said, those who do not remember the past are condemned to repeat it.

We know that war is an organized action of aggression or defense, planned in advance, carried out mainly by men but supported by women, and undertaken to achieve certain goals that have the approval of a tribe or nation. We know also that war is neither instinctive nor inevitable, and cannot exist without the approval of enough men and women—or boys and girls.

But the power that can come from understanding this, and from our understanding of the "good guy/bad guy" myth, requires awareness and judgment, as well as the courage to think independently. If we are to build the ramparts of peace, neither adults nor young people can afford to take the seemingly easy course of passive nonparticipation.

Young people can carefully study the news, applying their own judgments to events. They can seek to influence elected officials—on the local, state and national level—by writing or phoning to express opinions. They can discuss their views, and the reasons they hold them, with people old enough to vote. And they can urge the people who make decisions about news coverage at television stations, newspapers and magazines to provide expanded reporting of important issues.

We must all work to bring about change through nonviolent means. And, like Rosa Parks and all the followers of Gandhi and King, our best course is to work together. We can join with others in organizations that work for constructive change, particularly peace organizations. Ultimately, for both young people and adults, the most direct and effective action can be taken by working with others.

Many peace organizations came into being during the protests against the war in Vietnam. In fact, the outcome of that war might have been far more disastrous without them. Today, groups of all kinds—over 1,300 by the mid-1980s—have joined together to work for peace at local, national and international levels.

If we are to become a peaceful world, we must refuse to accept the counterfeit promises of the "good guy/bad guy" myth and instead learn to find glory in helping rather than condemning, conquering and destroying other people. We must begin to work, as individuals and as nations, for the kinds of changes needed to create a world where people can get along without "enemies."

Sources

1. Excellent examples of the multiple ways in which war can be studied will be found in R. A. Falk and S. S. Kim, eds., *The War System: An Interdisciplinary Approach* (1980) and in G. H. Snyder and P. Diesing, eds., *Conflict Among Nations: Bargaining, Decision Making, and System Structure in International Crises* (1977).

CHAPTER ONE. Myth and Reality

1. The analysis of mythic (as compared to philosophical or scientific) thinking presented in this chapter rests particularly on the work of H. Frankfort, *et al, Before Philosophy: The Intellectual Adventure of Ancient Man* (1973).

2. W.C.H. Laves and C. A. Thomson, *UNESCO: Purpose, Progress, Prospects* (1957), p. 415.

CHAPTER TWO. The Puzzle of War

1. See H. H. Turney-High, *Primitive War: Its Practice and Concepts* (1971), pp. 46ff.

2. See, for example, A. R. Buchanan, *The United States and World*

War II (1964) and K. Anderson, *Wartime Women: Sex Roles, Family Relations, and the Status of Women During World War II* (1981).

3. See B. Hacker, "Women and Military Institutions in Early Modern Europe," in *Signs. Journal of Women in Culture and Society* (1981) 6:4, pp. 643–71; and N. Goldman, ed., *Female Soldiers— Combatants or Noncombatants? Historical and Contemporary Perspectives* (1982). S. Saywell, *Women in War* (1985), and M. L. Rossiter, *Women in the Resistance* (1986), focus on the period since 1937. Nira Yuval-Davis, "Front and Rear: The Sexual Division of Labor in the Israeli Army," in *Feminist Studies* (1985) 11:3, pp. 649–76, is an interesting case study of shifting attitudes about the role of women in the military.

4. For two of the more sophisticated and cautious developments of this thesis, see K. Lorenz, *On Aggression*, trans. M. K. Wilson (1966), and E. O. Wilson, *On Human Nature* (1978).

5. Two of the finest analyses of men in battle are J. Keegan, *The Face of Battle* (1976), and J. G. Gray, *The Warriors: Reflections on Men in Battle* (1967). Among the numerous personal accounts available, C. B. MacDonald, *Company Commander* (1947), is particularly honest and straightforward.

6. See S.L.A. Marshall, *Men Against Fire: The Problem of Battle Command in Future War* (1956).

7. See J.G.D. Clark, *The Stone Age Hunter* (1967); R. B. Lee and I. de Vore, eds., *Man, the Hunter* (1968); and P. Shepard, *The Tender Carnivore and the Sacred Game* (1973).

8. See H. Breuil, *Four Hundred Centuries of Cave Art*, trans. M. E. Boyle (1952).

9. See J.G.D. Clark and S. Piggett, *Prehistoric Societies* (1965) and K. C. Chang, *The Archaeology of Ancient China* (1968).

CHAPTER THREE. Revenge and Magic

1. A. M. Hocart, *Kings and Councillors: An Essay in the Comparative Anatomy of Human Society* (1970), is an excellent discussion of the relations among human beings' desire for control, magic and human-institution building.

2. There is a multitude of anthropological books and scholarly articles on warring tribal societies. Among the more accessible are

R. Gardner and K. G. Heider, *Gardens of War* (1968); M. J. Harner, *The Jivaro: People of the Sacred Waterfalls* (1972); R. A. Rappaport, *A Pig for the Ancestors: Ritual in the Ecology of a New Guinea People* (1968), and R. M. Underhill, *Singing for Power: The Song Magic of the Papago Indians of Southern Arizona* (1973). *Dead Birds* (Phoenix Films, 1963) and *Ax Fight* (Documentary Educational Resources, 1977) are two excellent short films on tribal warfare.

3. See E. J. Krige, *The Social System of the Zulus* (1957).

4. See R. H. Lowie, *Indians of the Plains* (1954) and G. Dumezil, *The Destiny of the Warrior*, trans. G. Simpson (1964).

5. See P. Middelkoop, *Head Hunting in Timor and Its Historical Implications* (1963).

6. See R. J. Lifton, *Home from the War: Vietnam Veterans: Neither Victims nor Executioners* (1973) and *Interviews with My Lai Veterans* (New Yorker Films, 1971).

7. Quoted in translation in S. Keen, *Faces of the Enemy: Reflections of the Hostile Imagination* (1986), p. 30.

8. See N. A. Chagnon, *Yanomamo: The Fierce People* (1968).

9. See K. H. Basso and M. E. Opler, eds., *Apachean Culture, History and Ethnology* (1971); G. Goodwin, *Western Apache Raiding and Warfare* (1971); and M. E. Opler, *An Apache Life-way: The Economic, Social, and Religious Institutions of the Chiricahua Indians* (1965).

10. See C. M. Turnbull, *The Forest People* (1962).

11. See A. Balikci, *The Netsilik Eskimo* (1970).

12. See M. Shalins, *Stone Age Economics* (1972).

13. In addition to the material scattered throughout the books cited in note 2, see H. Barry, I. Child and M. K. Bacon, "The Relation of Child-Training to Subsistence Economy," *American Anthropologist* (1959) 61:51.

14. The psychological analysis presented in this book rests in particular on Gestalt psychology as developed by Fritz Perls. The most comprehensive statement of this theory is F. Perls, R. Hefferline and P. Goodman, *Gestalt Therapy: Excitement and Growth in the Human Personality* (1951), while the most readable introduction is F. Perls, *Gestalt Therapy Verbatim* (1969). See also S. Mansfield,

The Gestalts of War: An Inquiry into Its Origins and Meanings as a Social Institution (1982).

15. See A. Bullock, *Hitler: A Study in Tyranny* (1960) and G. Reitlinger, *The Final Solution: The Attempt to Exterminate the Jews of Europe, 1939–1945* (1961). The film *Night and Fog* (Filmmakers' Library, 1955) is a graphic evocation of the death camps.

16. "Man Has No 'Killer' Instinct," in M.F.A. Montagu, *Man and Aggression* (1968), p. 34. The film *Amish: A People of Preservation* (Encyclopaedia Britannica Education Corp., 1977) describes such a society.

CHAPTER FOUR. Wars of Greed and How They Began

1. See P. Green, *Alexander the Great* (1870); M. Renault, *The Nature of Alexander* (1975); and W. W. Tarn, *Alexander the Great* (1948–50).

2. See R. Coulborn, *The Origin of Civilized Societies* (1969).

3. There is a multitude of books, organized by continent, nation or century, that describe these wars. Two of the earliest and still among the finest are Thucydides, *The Peloponnesian War*, and Livy, *The History of Rome*: Both are available in several paperback translations. W. L. Langer, ed., *An Encyclopedia of World History* (1948), is also instructive. The book covers the period from 3000 B.C. to A.D. 1945 in 1,150 pages of small print and terse reporting: About 80 percent of the text is devoted to wars and peace treaties!

4. See in particular K. Horney, *The Neurotic Personality of Our Time* (1964).

5. See L. de Mause, ed., *The History of Childhood* (1974); R. Forster and O. Ranum, eds., *Family and Society* (1976); and S. A. Queen and R. W. Habenstein, *The Family in Various Cultures* (1967).

6. For a slightly different interpretation of the data, see A. Montagu, *Touching: The Human Significance of the Skin* (1971), and J. Prescott, "Body Pleasure and the Origins of Violence," *Bulletin of the Atomic Scientists* (November 1975) 31:9, 10–20.

7. See D. Hunt, *Parents and Children in History: The Psychology of Family Life in Early Modern France* (1970), which is based primarily on the well-documented childhood of Louis XIII.

8. See J. B. Wolf, *Louis XIV* (1968); G. P. Gooch, *Frederick the Great: The Ruler, the Writer, the Man* (1947); and J. M. Thompson, *Napoleon Bonaparte: His Rise and Fall* (1952). The short film *Battle of Culloden* (Filmmakers' Library, 1966) is one of the most accurate re-creations of a historic battle available.

CHAPTER FIVE. Of Joy and Honor

1. See K. Fowler, ed., *The Hundred Years War* (1971) and E. Perroy, *The Hundred Years' War* (1965).

2. Homer, *The Iliad*, trans. A. Lang, W. Leaf and E. Meyers, ed. G. Highet (1950), p. 382.

3. P. Teilhard de Chardin, *The Making of a Mind: Letters from a Soldier-Priest, 1914–1919* (1965), p. 205.

4. Quoted in S. M. Gilbert, "Soldier's Heart: Literary Men, Literary Women, and the Great War," in *Signs. Journal of Women in Culture and Society* (1983) 8:3, 439–40.

5. J. Froissart, *Chronicles of England, France, Spain, and the Adjoining Countries from the Latter Part of the Reign of Edward II to the Coronation of Henry IV*, trans. T. Johnes (1901), vol. 2, p. 347.

6. Homer, *op. cit.*, p. 158.

7. Froissart, *op. cit.*, pp. 1–2.

8. See Ivan Morris, *The Nobility of Failure: Tragic Heroes in the History of Japan* (1975).

9. M. Janowitz, *The Professional Soldier, A Social and Political Portrait* (1960), p. 22.

10. *Last Letters from Stalingrad*, trans. F. Schneider and C. Gullans (1965), pp. 36–38.

11. Homer, *op. cit.*, p. 458.

12. See M. Finley, *The World of Odysseus* (1965) and C.W.C. Oman, *The Art of War in the Middle Ages, A. D. 378–1515*, rev. and ed. J. H. Beeler (1953).

13. S.L.A. Marshall, *Men Against Fire* (1956), p. 22.

14. The statement, from a news briefing at the Pentagon in February 1971, is quoted in full in P. Dickson, *The Electronic Battlefield* (1976), p. 86.

15. This statement, made in a personal conversation with Sam Keen, 11 September 1985, is quoted in *Faces of the Enemy*, p. 82.

CHAPTER SIX. "New and Improved"—
How War Was Modernized

1. See E. A. Falk, *Togō and the Rise of Japanese Sea Power* (1936), for the only full biography of Togō in English.
2. Quoted in W. L. Neumann, *America Encounters Japan: From Perry to MacArthur* (1963), p. 31.
3. See D. Fieldhouse, *Colonialism, 1870–1945: An Introduction* (1981) and E. M. Winslow, *The Pattern of Imperialism: A Study in the Theories of Power* (1984).
4. For a good overview of the development of military technology and organizational efficiency, see W. H. McNeill, *The Pursuit of Power* (1982). J. U. Nef, *Western Civilization Since the Renaissance: Peace, War, Industry and the Arts* (1963) presents a different but equally important approach to the topic.
5. See M. Roberts, *The Military Revolution, 1560–1660* (1956).
6. For a case study of this development, see W. Goerlitz, *History of the German General Staff, 1657–1945* (1959).
7. See P. Paret, "Napoleon and the Revolution in War," in P. Paret, ed., *Makers of Modern Strategy from Machiavelli to the Nuclear Age* (1986).
8. See, for example, E. A. Pratt, *The Rise of Rail-Power in War and Conquest, 1833–1914* (1915), and D. Showalter, *Railroads and Rifles: Soldiers, Technology and the Unification of Germany* (1975).
9. See J. C. Stobart, *The Grandeur That Was Rome* (1961). M. Loewe, *Imperial China. The Historical Background to the Modern Age* (1969), provides similar data for another civilization.
10. For a discussion of this traditional view of time, see M. Eliade, *The Myth of the Eternal Return or, Cosmos and History* (1974).
11. See J. W. Burrow, *Evolution and Society: A Study in Victorian Social Theory* (1966).
12. Quoted in Neumann, *op. cit.*, p. 105.
13. This is a "translation" of Clausewitz by Ferdinand Foch, one

of the leading French generals and military theorists of the late nineteenth and early twentieth centuries. See F. Foch, *Principles of War*, trans. H. Belloc (1920), p. 44. Italics in the original. The Paret anthology cited in note 7 has several articles on the influence of Clausewitz on nineteenth-century military thought.

14. See, for example, L. L. Farrar, *The Short-War Illusion: German Policy, Strategy and Domestic Affairs, August–December 1914* (1973).

15. See A.J.P. Taylor, *The Struggle for Mastery in Europe, 1848–1918* (1954), and G. Ritter, *The Schlieffen Plan* (1958).

16. D. Macintyre, *The Thunder of the Guns: A Century of Battleships* (1960), is the most accessible of the various studies of naval development.

17. See Falk, *op. cit.*, p. 425.

18. *Ibid.*, p. 427.

CHAPTER SEVEN. Brutal Fear

1. See, for example, P. Fussell, *The Great War and Modern Memory* (1975), and R. Wohl, *The Generation of 1914* (1979).

2. V. Brittain, *Testament of Youth* (1933), p. 98.

3. C. E. Montague, *Disenchantment* (1968), p. 14.

4. See T. Ackworth, *Trench Warfare, 1914–1918: The Live and Let-Live System* (1980), and J. Ellis, *Eye-Deep in Hell: Trench Warfare in World War I* (1976). See also *Over There: 1914–1918* (New Yorker Films, 1963), which relies primarily on German and French newsreels, army propaganda films and footage shot by amateur soldier-cameramen.

5. See M. Hankey, *The Supreme Command, 1914–1919* (1961), for a discussion of strategic thinking, and A. Horne, *The Price of Glory: Verdun, 1916* (1963), for a battle of attrition.

6. The quotation is from a private letter to his fiancée, Vera Brittain, *op. cit.*, p. 198.

7. G. Chapman, *A Passionate Prodigality* (1966), pp. 133–134.

8. See M. Ferro, *The Great War, 1914–1918* (1973), for an excellent discussion of the impact of the war on European society.

9. B. H. Liddell Hart, *History of the Second World War* (1971), p. 37.

10. See A. Werth, *The Year of Stalingrad* (1947), and A. Clark, *Barbarossa: The Russian-German Conflict, 1941–1945* (1965). John Huston's documentary *The Battle of San Pietro* (Kit Parker Films, 1945) is one of the best studies of a World War II battle.

11. See D. Irving, *The Destruction of Dresden* (1963). See also *Hiroshima–Nagasaki, August 1945* (MOMA, 1945) and *Tale of Two Cities* (United States National Audiovisual Center, 1949).

12. S. B. Fay, *The Origins of the World War* (1920), vol. 2, pp. 185–86. Italics in original.

13. S. D. Sazonov, *Fateful Years, 1909–1916: The Reminiscences of Serge Sazonov* (1928), p. 201.

14. L. Albertini, *The Origins of the War of 1914*, trans. and ed. by I. M. Massey (1952–57), vol. 3, p. 407.

15. G. P. Gooch and H. Temperley, eds., *British Documents on the Origins of the War, 1898–14* (1926–38), vol. 2, p. 671.

16. See G. M. Trevelyan, *Grey of Fallodon: The Life and Letters of Sir Edward Grey* (1937). Grey was foreign minister in 1914.

17. H. Rauschning, *Hitler Speaks* (1939), pp. 125–26.

18. H. S. Truman, *Public Papers* (1951), p. 176.

19. *Ibid.*, p. 188.

20. *Report of the Central Committee of the Communist Party of the Soviet Union to the 20th Party Congress* (1956), Part I. For a scholarly discussion of the development of Soviet thinking about war, see C. Rice, "The Making of Soviet Strategy," in P. Paret, ed., *Makers of Modern Strategy from Machiavelli to the Nuclear Age,* (1986), pp. 648–676.

21. Sun Tzu, *The Art of War*, trans. S. B. Griffith (1963), ch. 2, sections 23, 33.

22. S. Keen, *Faces of the Enemy: Reflections of the Hostile Imagination* (1986), pp. 44–45.

23. *The New York Times*, April 28, 1982, Section I, p. 12.

CHAPTER EIGHT. The Terror of "Little Wars"

1. The best general work in English on the Algerian war is A. Horne, *A Savage War of Peace: Algeria, 1954–1962* (1978). *The Battle of Algiers* is an excellent and unusual re-creation of the terrorist

campaign: Saadi Yacef, one of the 1956 fighters, was one of the producers of the film and played himself in it!

2. The best introductions to the history of guerrilla warfare are J. Ellis, *A Short History of Guerrilla Warfare* (1975) and W. Laqueur, *The Guerrilla Reader: A Historical Anthology* (1977). The most comprehensive is R. B. Asprey, *War in the Shadows: The Guerrilla in History* (1975). *Tupamaros* (Unifilm, 1972) covers the history, strategy and ideology of an Uruguayan urban guerrilla force.

3. Old Testament, I Samuel 22:2.

4. Apochrypha, II Maccabees 8:7.

5. See C. Rougeron, "The Historical Dimension of Guerrilla Warfare," in G. Chaliand, ed., *Guerrilla Strategies: An Historical Anthology from the Long March to Afghanistan* (1982).

6. See G. C. Herring, *America's Longest War: The United States and Vietnam, 1950–1975* (1979), for a short but balanced introduction to the war. J. Race, *War Comes to Long An* (1972), is a good case study of American counterguerrilla tactics.

7. See Vo Nguyen Giap, *People's War, People's Army* (1962), for a discussion of guerrilla strategy by a successful guerrilla leader, and H. Blanco, *Land or Death: The Peasant Struggle in Peru* (1962), for the thoughtful self-criticism of an unsuccessful guerrilla leader.

8. See W. Laqueur, *Terrorism: A Study of National and International Political Violence* (1977).

9. See C. Carlton, *Bigotry and Blood* (1977). *Tale of Two Irelands* (CBS News, 1975) examines the civil war in Ireland by focusing on two militant young men, one Protestant and the other Catholic.

10. *The War in Algeria* (1961) quoted in Horne, *op. cit.*, p. 55.

11. See J. P. Harrison, *The Endless War: Vietnam's Struggle for Independence* (1982). *Ho Chi Minh* (MacMillan Films, 1966) contains some interesting footage on this very successful guerrilla leader.

12. J. V. Moore, "The Modern Grapes of Wrath. World's Methodists Told of South Africa's 'State Thuggery,' " in *Sacramento Bee*, October 11, 1986, p. B5. Moore deliberately does not publish the woman's name in order to protect her against possible reprisals in South Africa.

13. See H. C. D'Eucausse, *Decline of an Empire: The Soviet So-*

cialist Republics in Revolt (1987), for a case study of the limits of repression and oppression.

14. See A. Guillen, "Urban Guerrilla Strategy," in Chaliand, *op. cit.*, pp. 317–23.

15. Moore, *op. cit.*

16. For a good, scholarly introduction to the civil rights movement, see H. Sitkoff, *The Struggle for Black Equality: 1954–1980* (1981). *Sit-in* (McGraw-Hill Films, 1961) documents the first lunch-counter sit-ins in Nashville, as well as the training in peaceful resistance given participants.

17. Quoted in J. Harris, *The Long Freedom Road* (1967), p. 41.

18. M. B. Green, *The Origins of Non-Violence: Tolstoy and Gandhi in Their Historical Settings* (1986), is a good introduction to the history of nonviolent techniques and philosophy. The actual words of Gandhi can be studied in the following works: *The Moral and Political Writings of Mahatma Gandhi*, ed. R. Iyer (1985); *The Essential Gandhi*, ed. L. Fischer (1962). See also M. L. King, Jr., *Stride Toward Freedom* (1958); *Why We Can't Wait* (1964); and *Where Do We Go from Here: Chaos or Community* (1967). *Dr. Martin Luther King, Jr. . . . An Amazing Grace* (McGraw-Hill Films, 1978) focuses on several of King's most famous speeches; the very fine commercial film *Gandhi* is now available on videotape.

19. Harris, *op. cit.*

20. See N. Downs, ed., *Basic Documents in Medieval History* (1959), pp. 73–76.

21. See P. Tillich, *The Courage to Be* (1964), p. 50.

22. See G. Sharp, *Making Europe Unconquerable: The Potential of Civilian-Based Deterrence and Defense* (1987) for a provocative analysis of how massive, nonviolent resistance could be used to preserve European independence.

CHAPTER NINE. Building the Ramparts of Peace

1. Quoted in S. Keen, *Faces of the Enemy: Reflections of the Hostile Imagination* (1986), p. 31.

2. From an article in *Protestant Telegraph*, May 31, 1969, quoted in C. Carlton, *Bigotry and Blood* (1977), p. 88.

3. Translated in H. Schwartz, *Tsars, Mandarins and Commissars: A History of Chinese-Russian Relations* (1973), p. 248.

4. *Ibid.*, p. 245.

5. S. Koch, *op. cit.*, p. 22.

6. D. S. Broder, "Stockman: Blame Boss for Deficits," *Sacramento Bee*, December 27, 1986, p. A8.

7. "Federal Spending Report," *UC* [University of California] *Clip Sheet* (November 18, 1986) 62:10, 1.

8. M. Meltzer, *Ain't Gonna Study War No More* (1985), p. 260.

Appendix:

Peace Organizations

The following organizations may be contacted for information about their affiliates (or similar organizations) in specific communities:

Beyond War (formerly Creative Initiative)
222 High Street
Palo Alto, CA 94301-1097
(415) 328-7756

Citizens Against Nuclear War
1201 16th Street NW
Washington, DC 20036
(202) 822-7483

Consortium on Peace Research, Education and Development
University of Illinois
911 West High Street, Room 100
Urbana, IL 61801
(217) 333-2069

Jobs with Peace Campaign
76 Summer Street
Boston, MA 02110
(617) 338-5783

Physicians for Social Responsibility
1601 Connecticut Avenue NW
Washington, DC 20009
(202) 939-5750

Union of Concerned Scientists
26 Church Street
Cambridge, MA 02238
(617) 547-5552

War Resisters League
339 Lafayette Street
New York, NY 10012
(212) 228-0450

Women's International League for Peace and Freedom
1213 Race Street
Philadelphia, PA 19107
(215) 563-7110

For further listings, check *American Peace Directory, 1984*, edited by Melinda Fine and Peter Steven.

Suggestions for Further Reading

Baldwin, Gordon C. *The Apache Indians: Raiders of the Southwest.* Four Winds, 1978.

Bender, David L., ed. *The Arms Race: Opposing Viewpoints.* Greenhaven Press, 1982.

Bentley, Judith. *The Nuclear Freeze Movement.* F. Watts, 1984.

Blumberg, Rhoda. *Commodore Perry in the Land of the Shogun.* Lothrop, 1985.

Carroll, Raymond. *The Palestine Question.* F. Watts, 1983.

Carter, Peter. *Mao.* Viking, 1979.

Cheney, Glenn Alan. *Mohandas Gandhi.* F. Watts, 1983.

———. *Revolutions in Central America.* F. Watts, 1984.

Claypool, J. *Hiroshima and Nagasaki.* F. Watts, 1984.

Coker, Christopher. *Terrorism.* F. Watts, 1986.

Connolly, Peter. *The Greek Armies.* Silver Burdett, 1980.

Coolidge, Olivia. *The Trojan War.* Houghton Mifflin, 1952.

Cowan, Lore. *Children of the Resistance.* Meredith Press, 1969.

Dolan, Edward. *Adolf Hitler: A Portrait in Tyranny.* Dodd, Mead, 1981.

Dupuy, T. N. *Stalemate in the Trenches.* F. Watts, 1967.

Everett, Susanne. *World War I: An Illustrated History.* Rand McNally, 1980.

Feldbaum, Carl B., and Ronald J. Bee. *Looking the Tiger in the Eye: Confronting the Nuclear Threat.* Harper & Row, 1988.

Firoozi, Edith, and I. Klein. *The Age of Great Kings.* Western Publishing Company, 1966.

Goode, Ruth. *People of the Ice Age.* Crowell-Collier, 1973.

Harris, Jacqueline. *Martin Luther King, Jr.* F. Watts, 1983.

Krensky, Stephen. *Conqueror and Hero: The Search for Alexander.* Little, Brown, 1981.

Lauré, Jason, and Ettagale Lauré. *South Africa: Coming of Age under Apartheid.* Farrar, Straus, 1980.

Lawson, D. *An Album of World War II: Home Fronts.* F. Watts, 1980.

Lens, Sidney. *The Bomb.* Lodestar Books, 1982.

Lewis, Brenda. *Growing Up in Samurai Japan.* David & Charles, 1981.

Masters, A. *Napoleon.* McGraw-Hill, 1981.

Meltzer, Milton, *Ain't gonna study war no more,* Harper & Row, 1985.

Meyer, Carolyn. *Voices of Northern Ireland: Growing Up in a Troubled Land.* Harcourt, 1987.

Miguel, Pierre. *The days of knights and castles.* Silver Burdett, 1980.

Raynor, Thomas P. *Terrorism: Past, Present, Future.* F. Watts, 1987.

Rink, Paul. *Quest for Freedom: Bolivar and the South American Revolution.* Messner, 1968.

Rossel, Seymour. *The Holocaust.* F. Watts, 1981.

Snyder, L. L., and I. M. Brown. *Frederick the Great: Prussian Warrior and Statesman.* F. Watts, 1968.

Syme, Ronald. *Garibaldi: The Man Who Made a Nation.* Morrow, 1967.

Uden, Grant. *Hero Tales from the Age of Chivalry: Retold from the Froissart Chronicles.* World Publishing, 1969.

Wilkinson, Burke. *Young Louis XIV: The Early Years of the Sun King.* Macmillan (New York), 1970.

Index

Achilles, 93, 98–99, 101, 103–4, 189
Adams, Samuel, 165
Afghanistan, 160–61
agriculture. *See* farming societies
airplanes, 105; unmanned, 108;
    World War II bombing, 138–39
Alexander the Great, 76–77, 87–
    88, 123, 130, 145, 151, 189; and
    material things, 82–84; Persian
    wars, 60–71; rebellion and, 159
Algeria: French attitudes toward,
    163, 170–71; guerrilla war and lib-
    eration, 153–56, 159, 161; and
    prudence, 168
ambushes, 39, 155–56, 157, 159
American Revolution, 158–61
Americans, 16–17, 85; and Boston
    Tea Party, 158; "can-do" approach
    to problems, 104
anger and rage: babies and, 26; and
    creation myths, 48–49; farming
    societies and child rearing, 51–54;
    government oppression and vio-
    lence, 172–73, 180–81; hunting-
    and-gathering societies, 50–51;

industrial societies, 147–48,
    151–52
animals, 78; instinctive behavior of,
    26; Cro-Magnon pictures of, 30
Apache Indians, 57–58. *See also*
    Chiricahua Apaches
archaeology, 29–31, 36
aristocracy, 71, 74–77
Aristotle, 32, 170
armies: Alexander and Darius, 61–
    69; development of states, 72, 74,
    76; expansion and military drafts,
    127; and industrial revolution, 122;
    modern, and computerized war-
    fare, 108–9; professional, 29, 74–
    76; pyramidal organization of, 79
assassinations, 140, 153, 164, 177
assimilation process, 169–71
atomic bomb, 139
Austro-Hungarian Empire, 130, 135,
    140
Azedine, Si, 155–56

babies: and stork myth, 11–13; anger
    and, 26

Ludendorff, General Erich Wilhelm von, 22

Maccabees, 157–58
MacFarlane, Charles, 111
machine guns, 132–34
magic, and war: neolithic tribes and, 37–44
Magnum, Senator Willie, 111
Mao Ze-dong, 162
Marcos, Ferdinand and Imelda, 77
Marlborough, Duke of, 16–17
Marshall, S.L.A., 28, 105
masculinity: characteristic of war, 23–24; and neolithic customs, 38–45
mass times speed theory, 126, 132, 138
materialism, 81–82
medieval era, 104–5, 181–82
Meltzer, Milton, 190
mercenary soldiers, 76
military: adherence to heroic code and, 98–105; and differing battle strategies, 16–19; and industrial revolution, 122; organizational changes and bureaucracy, 120–21; and soldiers' fear of killing, 27–29; and study of war, 2
missiles, 105
mobilization, 127–28, 140–41
Mohammed, 181
Moltke, Helmuth von, 141
Montague, C.E., 131–32
Montgomery, Alabama, 174–76, 193
Moore, Reverend John V., 172–73
Mountbatten, Lord Louis, 164
movies, 6–9, 187
muskets, 112, 119
Muslims, 155, 158; Pope Urban and, 181–82. *See also* Islam
myths: and community action, 12–14; and emotional truth, 10–13; *See also* "good guy/bad guy" myth

Napoleon, 121, 126, 156
National Association for the Advancement of Colored People (NAACP), 175

navies, 122, 128–29
Nazi regime, 57, 102, 157, 165–67. *See also* Hitler, Adolf
Near East, 31, 63, 126; and guerrillas, 158
neolithic civilization, 31–32; causes of war and creation myths, 46–49, 148; magic rituals of war, 37–44; and personality, 54–58; and sharing of goods, 78–79; and warfare, 58, 71, 75, 188–89. *See also* farming societies
neutral states, 151
Nicaragua, 161
Nixon, Richard, 186
Nobel, Alfred, 119
nobility: French, at Poitiers, 90, 92, 95, 97–99, 103; French, at Battle of Crécy, 88–90, 98–99, 101, 105; medieval holy wars and, 182
"No-man's-land," 27, 133
nonviolence, 175–85, 194
nuclear war, 139; and denial of reality, 190; public approval and consent for, 34–35; and weaponry, 145

Ojibway Indians, 46, 72; magic ritual and war, 36–39; and type of warfare, 15–20, 68; war weapon of, 31
oppression, 180–81

Palestine: guerrillas, 161; Maccabee rebellion, 157–58
Papago Indians, 57
Parks, Rosa, 174–75, 193, 194
patriarchy, 80–81
Patton, General George, 108
peace: myths of war and, 14; organizations for, 194–95; and preparedness for war, 8–9
peasants: and material goods, 82–83; and rebellion, 76, 156–57, 159; as soldiers, 29
Periboriwa, 47–48, 100
Perry, Admiral Matthew, 111–12
Persia, 145; Alexander's conquest of, 60–71; nobility of, 80
Philip, King of France, 88–90
Pogo, 183

Poitiers, Battle of, 90–92, 95, 99;
Edward's speech, 97–98, 102
Poland, 139, 151
popular support for wars, 19–24, 33–
35, 194; and World War I, 139–42
Portugal, 121
prejudice, 180
preparedness, 8–9, 19–21, 24, 188–
90; costs of, 188–89; and 19th-
century beliefs, 129
progress, theory of, 124–25, 131,
146, 150–51, 188
projection, 56–59, 148–49, 152; self-
love compared to self-hate, 177,
180–84
propaganda: dictators and, 33; and
guerrilla tactics, 163; Soviet compared to American, 187; during
wartime, 147–48
Protestants, 182
prudence/loyalty conflicts, 165–72
psychology: of fear, and modern
weapons, 145; of love, 177, 180;
modern war customs and, 39; neolithic compared to modern warfare, 39; neolithic understanding of
killing, 44–45; and projection, 56–
57; prudence/loyalty conflict and
stress, 167; and study of war, 3–4
public opinion: and guerrilla warfare,
162–64. See also popular support
for wars
Pygmies, 50

"queer bashing," 183

racism: and nonviolent protest, 174–
77; in World War II, 148
Rambo films, 187
Reagan, Ronald, 151; arms buildup,
189
religion, 34; and fanaticism, 181–82;
and guerrilla resistance, 156–58,
168–69; and neolithic warfare, 37–
44, 148–49
revenge, 6–7, 13, 46; and changes in
family structure, 50–56, 58, 79
Revere, Paul, 162, 165
revolutions, 76; after World War I,
135; and prudence vs. group loy-

alty, 167–68. See also specific up-
risings
Roman Empire, 29, 32, 157; and
conquered people, 168–69; and just
wars, 123–24
Roosevelt, Franklin D., 148, 180
Roosevelt, Theodore, 128–29, 189
Roy, Jules, 170
Russia, 22, 135; invasions of, 121,
138; and World War II, 139. See
also Soviet Union; World War I

sacrifices: and Alexander, 70; and
pursuit of wealth and greed, 77; in
wartime, 20–23
samurai, 29, 101, 110, 112–17, 123
Sandinistas, 168
Saul, King, 157
Sazonov, Serge, 140
science, 13; and 19th-century weaponry, 118–19; and objective truth,
10; and study of war, 1–2
Serbia, 140
Shalins, Martin, 52
Sinclair, Mary, 94
Sioux Indians, 15–18
slavery, 32–33
soldiers: anger and killing, 26–29;
mercenary and professional, 74–
76, 96–97; in modern times, 105–
9; and peacetime draft, 127, 131;
pleasure of war and "joy of battle," 92–97; training of, 27–29,
119–20; in trenches during World
War I, 132–35
South Africa, 154; blacks and rage,
172–74
South Vietnam, 107, 160
Soviet Union, 34, 104, 149–50; and
Afghan guerrillas, 159–61; and
Chinese, 186–87; and female sol-
diers, 23; and United States, 148,
186–87; and war preparedness, 20,
144. See also Russia
Spain, 32, 121, 156, 169
Stalin, Joseph, 34
Star Trek stories, 187
Star Wars films, 187
"Star Wars" (Strategic Defense Initi-
ative), 189

states, nation, 71–74
Stockman, David, 189
stories of adventure, 6–9, 187–88.
See also myths
stork myth, 11–13
Strategic Defense Initiative (SDI),
189
Sun, Tzu, 145
"survival of the fittest" theory, 125,
146, 150–51, 169

taxes, 21; creation of state and armies, 71, 72, 74, 76
technology: and computerized warfare, 107–9; and international relations, 150–51; and weaponry, 118–
19
Teilhard de Chardin, Pierre, 93–94
territory. *See* greed, wars of
terrorism, 140, 190; and Algerian
guerrillas, 153–55; theatricality and
hostage taking, 154, 163–64. *See
also* guerrilla warfare
Tillich, Paul, 182
Tito, Josip Broz, 165, 168
TNT, 119
training, army: and discipline, 120;
of soldiers to kill, 17–19
transportation systems, 127, 139,
151, 163
trench warfare, 27, 132–35
Trojan War, 93, 98–99, 103–4
Truman, Harry, 143
Tunisia, 161
Turkey, 63, 143

UNESCO (United Nations Educational, Scientific, and Cultural Organization), 14
United Nations, 33, 162
United States, 71, 117; and American
Revolution, 165; attitudes toward
enemy, 147–48; and Central
America, 161; civil rights movement and, 174–80, 185; "domino
theory," 143; and hostage taking,
164; immigrants and group identi-
fication, 166; and Japan, 85, 125;
leaders and war, 186–93; and military bureaucracy, 120; and military

expenditures, 19–20; and revolution, 158–60; and slavery, 32–33;
and Soviets, 186–87; Supreme
Court school segregation case, 174;
and Vietnam War, 44–45, 107–8,
160; and World War I, 130; and
world wars, 45
Urban II, Pope, 181–82
Uruguay, 173

Versailles Peace Conference, 171
victory: *mass times speed* equals, 126,
132; with new war machines,
138
Vietnam, 143, 164; and Ho Chi
Minh, 170–71; War, 106–7, 160,
194–95; veterans of War, 44–45
violence, 9, 14, 58; and government
provocation, 172–74; inevitability
of, and heroism, 102; nonviolent
resistance and, 176–77, 184–85.
See also guerrilla warfare

Wallace, George, 174
war: changes in meaning and value,
123–25; essential characteristics,
18–24, 193–94; as instinctive, 24,
26–29, 32, 35, 194; limits to, 42–
44, 75, 190; modern computerized,
106–9; studies of, 1–4. *See also*
fear, wars of; greed, wars of; guerrilla warfare
wealth, 72, 74. *See also* greed
weapons, 19–20; Cro-Magnon era,
30–31; of Japanese navy, 19th century, 112–18; legal ownership of,
29; new and electronic, 105, 107–
9; 19th-century advances and
standardization, 118–19, 128; and
nuclear war, 34–35; in Persian
wars, 62; in World War I, 132
Western films, 6–7, 187
women: and heroic tradition, 101;
neolithic, and war rituals, 38–39,
43–44; new independence and,
191; political inferiority of, 32; as
soldiers, 23–24; and war effort,
20–21
World War I, 45, 94, 171, 189;
beginning of, 130–32, 139–42;